FROM ONE PSYCHIC TO ANOTHER:

Advice & Teachings For The Newly Awaken Psychic In You

SUE M. SWANK

Copyright © 2016 SUE M. SWANK

All rights reserved.

ISBN -10: 1539793532
ISBN-13: 978-1539793533

BOOK COVER PHOTOGRAPHY BY: SUE M. SWANK

DEDICATION

I want to dedicate this to everyone, who is stumbling along their spiritual path…hang in there kiddies…it will make sense in time.

CONTENTS

1	BUSINESS MATTERS	1
2	FOUNDATION OF RULES & ETHICS	10
3	MEDITATION, MEDITATION, MEDITATION	16
4	SHIELDING	26
5	MANIFESTING YOUR ABILITIES	34
6	YOUR GUIDES	45
7	GIVING READINGS	50
8	PSYCHICS & BOUNDARIES	69
9	SKEPTICS & DEBRIEFING AFTER A READING	76
10	FINAL THOUGHTS	82

A WORD FROM THE AUTHOR...

Hello, I'm Sue M. Swank.

One night I was going through my vast collection of teachings that I have given over the years and decided to place them in a book, so that for those who are new to their psychic abilities can read and perhaps take something away from each lesson.

In this book, you will read some of my past experiences, mixed with some of my teachings.
Enjoy it...
Learn from it...
Most of all...
Understand that only you can walk your spiritual path...

The rest of us can only watch.

<3 Be real...be blessed <3

Sue M. Swank

1 BUSINESS MATTERS

PSYCHICS, MEDIUMS, PSYCHIC MEDIUMS & THE LAW

As you explore your spirituality path, you learn about how to take care of yourself (your aura/chakras/overall well-being/etc.), you learn how to communicate with your guides, as well as those in the afterlife, etc. What isn't thoroughly discussed or review extensively is the legal system and you, as a psychic, medium, or a psychic medium.

Every person who enters the world of psychics, mediums, psychic mediums, has to possess the basic understanding of the legal system and how it relates to what they are doing (even if it is for a hobby). Ignorance in the eyes of the law is not an acceptable defense in today's courtroom.

Areas that psychics, mediums and psychic mediums should research, understand and be educated about are as follows:
- Business Licenses
- Medical Advice/Diagnoses
- Slander .Liability
- Law Enforcement (Crimes, Etc.) & Admissible Evidence

BUSINESSES LICENSES:

Each state varies in their requirement for operating a psychic business (even if you are running your business as a hobby, be sure to research your states definition of "hobby" under running a business to see if you fall within that category).

MOST states (and counties) will require a psychic, medium and/or a psychic medium to have a valid business license. This includes their DBA (doing business as) and their tax I.D. number (most often their social security number).

In SOME areas (such as Southern Nevada/Las Vegas), you must have a criminal background check (and be fingerprinted) in order to obtain a psychic arts license (there are some loopholes and exceptions within this requirement, so diligent research is required on your part).

When traveling to a different state to perform at an event, it is advisable for you to contact that states business license department as a soon as possible to verify whether or not you need a state or county license/permit for them as well

When in doubt, it is always encouraged that you contact your local state and county business license department and speak to them directly.

The penalties for operating a business (as defined by your state and county) without a license are steep, ranging from fines/penalties to possible jail time.

MEDICAL ADVICE/DIAGNOISES:

There comes a time when all psychics, mediums and/or psychic mediums will be privy to intimate medical conditions/issues within a certain person. The dilemma is to whether or not to inform that person of what you "feel".

While each state has their own individual regulations that pertain to the practice of medicine, generally one is considered to be practicing medicine if they are:
- Diagnose a medical condition
- Attempt to treat a medical condition (including surgery)
- Offer medicines, etc.
- Giving medical examinations
- Offering medical advice

Some of the areas that is NOT included:
- Selling books pertaining to medicine, nutrition, self-help, etc. & vitamins
- Healing (Reiki, yoga, meditation, etc.)

If you "feel" a certain medical condition applies to a certain person and you chose to inform that person of what you feel, understand that you are then placing yourself in the category of "diagnosing a medical condition". This can be interpreted as "Practicing medicine without a license".

You then risk liability charges, as well as county/state charges of:
• Operating a business with no business license or insurance
Federal charges including felony criminal charges:
• Practicing without a medical license
• Criminal manslaughter (involuntarily or voluntarily)
Not to mention personal civil lawsuits from the person and/or their surviving family members for:
• Loss of wages/incomes
• Financial, physical, or psychological harm

SLANDER/LIABILITY

Slander is defined as any false statements/verbiage spoken about a certain person that stands the risk of causing reputation damage.

Liable is defined as any statement or reference given in writing about a person that stands the risk of reputation damage.

Whenever a psychic, medium and/or a psychic medium gives a reading about an absent third party (spouse, partner, friend, business acquaintance, etc.), they stand the risk of slander/liability backwash if the information they receive is presented within a negative and/or unflattering manner.

■■■

Case example:

Psychic: Hi! Thank you for booking me today! How can I help you?
Client: I want to know about my husband and my best friend. They have been sneaky for this last month and I want to know what is going on.
Psychic: Ok, give me your wedding ring and let me focus (closes their eyes for a few moments, then opens and begins to talk): Is your friend Barbara?
Client: Yes.
Psychic: Is your husband Keith?
Client: Yes. What do you see them doing!
Psychic (closes their eyes and focuses some more then opens and talks): I'm seeing a large boat, like a cruise ship and now I see them in a hotel room, walking around it, looking at the view outside on the balcony. They look happy. Now I see them in a jewelry store, looking at something-
Client (upset): Oh my god! Are they having an affair with each other?!

Psychic (leans over and hands the ring back to the client and says): Yes. I know this for a fact they are having an affair. I'm so sorry but it is better you know this now and leave them both! You deserve better! Once a cheater ALWAYS a cheater!

The session ends with the client going home in tears, packing her clothes and leaving. While on her way out of the area, she contacts her attorney to begin divorce proceedings.

Later it was discovered that the husband enlisted the help of his wife's best friend to help create a romantic weekend get-away on a cruise ship that also included an overnight hotel stay at a 5-star hotel and a new diamond necklace they both picked out.

■■

It is vital that if you, as a psychic medium and/or a psychic medium attempt to read a third party without their consent (which is not advisable to many, however some elect to do so), that you refrain from accusing that third party of unflattering activities. To do so willingly, is to run the risk of potential slander/liability charges (which whether they hold up in a court of law or not doesn't matter because by that point the local media would have gotten the scoop on this and you just might find yourself on their radar for "news".

LAW ENFORCEMENT(CRIMES, ETC.) &ADMISSABLE EVIDENCE

The allure of assisting the police in a case is a strong drug for some psychics & psychic mediums. There's the thrill of "seeing" the crime as it unfolds in your mind, the feel of being "important & needed" by the law enforcement personnel in a certain case.

The one thing to understand is that YOU do not solve the case. YOU are a tool, in which the police department has elected to utilize because they are out of leads and have nowhere else to turn to. YOU are their last resort.

While there are some law enforcement agencies (whether inside certain departments, etc.) that do utilize psychics and psychic mediums, there are far more law enforcement agencies that will not and DO NOT actively entertain the notion of using a psychic, psychic medium at all Ever.

There are two reasons why they will not and do not ever use them:
• For every "valid" psychic, psychic medium worth their grain of salt, there are (at the minimum) 20+ self-proclaimed psychics and psychic

mediums who are frauds & fakes. They are in it for the $$$ and glory (ego) only
• Any and ALL information given to law enforcement by a psychic, psychic medium is NOT allowed to be submitted in court (prosecuting attorneys simply cannot include whatever information from the psychic, psychic medium as "admissible evidence"

So why even bother contacting law enforcement about a vison you feel might have some connection to a case they are working on?

Because you might have some valid insight to provide to them, this could result in more productive leads on their side, this solving the case.

Remember though, YOU do NOT solve a criminal case. LAW ENFOREMENT does. But that doesn't mean that you cannot be used as a tool in their investigation (ONLY when they are open to the concept of using a psychic, psychic medium).

STARTING & OPERATING YOUR BUSINESS AS A PSYCHIC

Owning and operating a business is always an ego boost. You call the shots, you plan your work schedule, etc. But how do you do it? Where do you start?

First you ask yourself these 2 questions:
1. Do I want to start my own business?
2. Can I run my own business effectively?

The answer will always be a yes or no. For those who answer yes to #1, then "maybe" to #2, then your answer is "no" for right now.

If your answer is "no", ask yourself why is it "no" right now? Do you feel you need more knowledge and experience? If so, the seek out every possible opportunity to gain more knowledge and experience and then revisit the business concept perhaps 6 months later to see if your answer has changed or not.

If your answer to #2 was a "I believe I can!" or "I want to try!" then your answer is a "yes".

THE BIG QUESTIONS!!!

The five biggest questions for anyone who is starting their own business are:
- Where do I start?
- Do I need a license?
- What should I use as my business name?
- How much should I charge?
- What about advertising? How do I get my business name out there to the public?

THE FIRST TWO QUESTIONS PERTAINING TO START AND IF YOU NEED A LICENSE can easily be found within your state statues/laws concerning businesses. This can be easily googled by typing in "How to get a business license in XXXX (type in whatever state you currently reside in). Once you do that, you should the name and phone number of the office where you should call and ask them directly as well (especially if you are trying to operate a business as a psychic).

THE THIRD QUESTION PERTAINS TO NAMING YOUR BUISNESS (and this might have also been answered in your call to the state business license office). They might have advised you to register as a "DBA" (Doing Business As). This is where you name your business. If registering your DBA, then be sure to keep records of ALL income and outcome finances to send in one a regular basis, so that you can pay taxes on these, etc.

When you create a business name, you want it to sound strong and realistic. As a psychic you want to steer clear from descriptive words such as "Amazing", "Prophet", "Mother/Father", etc. You also want to steer clear from descriptive titles such as "Psychic Betty-Lou, mother and seer of all", etc. These name do nothing to help generate business for you, in fact more often than not they will deter clients.

In many instances, placing a simple "Psychic" or "Psychic Medium" in front of your own name is actually more efficient business wise.

THE FOURTH QUESTION CENTERS AROUND HOW MUCH TO CHARGE. This is always a tricky question. It is tricky because if you charge too much, nobody can afford you. If you charge too little, then you are cheating yourself, thus not only devaluing your business, but your services as well.

In order to figure out what prices to charge, etc., take time to review websites from other psychics and see how they describe their services and their fees, then go from there. The outcome you want is a golden number (meaning a fee that is reasonable and fits the services that you are offering, without going over the top or devaluing your services overall).

The average rule of thumb when it comes to charging is: If you are getting booked throughout the week to where you have to have a schedule book and work your daily routine around your clients, then you should be charging for your services.

THE FIFTH QUESTION IS ALL ABOUT ADVERTISING. How to do it, where to start, etc. The age of the internet has changed not only everything about how we communicate with each other, but how we do business now as well.

The internet is not only a strong communication tool, it is also a powerful business tool and it is FREE. At the touch of your fingers, you can reach out to millions of people worldwide. Effective advertising begins and ends on the internet.

First you will want to create a website. Using your search engine (google in most cases), you can locate dozens of free website hosting places to choose from.

Keep in mind that you will be sub hosting from these sites, meaning that whatever you use as your domain name, it will also have: .wix.com or .weebly.com or .yola.com, etc. after it:
- Wix.com
- Weebly.com
- Yola.com
- Moonfruit.com
- SiteBuilder.com
- WebsiteBuilder.com

For those who are OK with paying a nominal fee for a site (without having to sub host (in other words your domain will only be yours), these are some websites to explore and consider:
- Godaddy.com
- Vistaprint.com
- Squarespace.com
- Sitey.com
- eHost.com

No matter site you choose, be sure that it feels right to you and that it fits with your business image overall.

Once your website is ready and published, you'll want to promote it. Social media is the bomb full stop. You have the top two social media sites offer premium client to business owner ration on this planet:
- Facebook.com
- Twitter.com

These two sites alone can make or break your business within a six-twelve month timeframe. No lie. Plus they are 100% FREE.

For FACEBOOK:
- Create a page for your business (using your business name)
- Join groups where you are allowed to promote your business
- Direct traffic to your business page by posting on it regularly
- Allow others to respond to you on your page

FOR TWITTER:
- Get an account
- Look for others who are I the same business as you (or those who are interested in what you do) and follow them (also allow them to follow you)
- Connect your Facebook with your twitter account (meaning when you post in one, it automatically posts to the other)

VERY VITAL:
- Be sure to post a link to your website on both Facebook and Twitter
- Be sure to create a blog and post this on both Facebook and Twitter
- Communicate, communicate, communicate

OTHER FORMS OF ADVERTISMENTS:
- Get business cards (vitsaprint.com is useful and often economical) and leave them around town (restrooms, on top of your tip when leaving a restaurants, community boards in your grocery store, etc.
- Attend community events and introduce yourself
- Consider offering a brief class and/or seminar at your local health food store
- Allow your friend to brag about you and your services (word of mouth does wonders)
- Make an announcement in your local paper offering your services, etc.
- Do interviews and have someone write something about you (be sure to provide your business name and website link as well!)

FINAL WORDS:

Owning a business can be a positive choice. HOWEVER, you must be VERY mindful about your time and energy. You cannot book clients after clients after clients, THEN work on your advertisement, THEN write a blog, THEN post on social media websites, THEN do whatever household chores you need to do (cook dinner, clean house, etc.), THEN schedule more clients, after clients, THEN have time for your family and yourself, THEN expect to go to bed peacefully, ALL in one day. You will burn out before you have given yourself a fair chance s running a business.

You need to pace yourself and plan everything out effectively. Select one day a week to do your required paperwork (whether for taxes, blogging, etc.), and pick (at least) one day a week to completely shut down and give yourself some much needed "quiet time" (this will help you to recharge yourself).

Good luck!

2 FOUNDATION OF RULES AND ETHICS

ETHICS & PSYCHICS

Psychics & Psychic Mediums have been labeled different names such as "Seer", "Fortune Teller", "Soothsayer", "gypsy", with some of the more unpleasant labels are "Scam artists", "Frauds", "Satan Worshippers", "Magician", etc. since the term "Psychic" existed.

In 2005, a Gallup Survey, from Princeton, New Jersey, revealed that 55% of the people reported that they believed in psychic or spiritual healing or the power of the human mind to heal the body. They estimated that approximately three out of four Americans believed in the paranormal overall:

http://www.gallup.com/poll/16915/three-four-americans-believe-paranormal.aspx

With so many people experiencing various "awakening" stages, stemming from extreme tragedy and chaos such as (NDE) Near Death Experience, trauma/illness, etc. It really is not difficult to understand the need to label something, to pigeon-hole it, analyze and dissect it seven ways for Sunday. It is within our human DNA to be as logical as possible, when encountering something that is unexplainable.

Finding a psychic/psychic medium is not hard at all. Go to any social media and you'll see them in groups, websites, etc. Every town has them in fact you would be very hard pressed NOT to find a psychic/psychic medium in your area.

The question then opens up to:
- Which psychic is honest & reputable?
- How do I know if I have a real psychic?

While there are some blatant red flags such as:
- Saying that you have a curse put on you (or your family/loved one) and it will take $$$ to remove it
- Saying that you have to buy a certain candle and/or oils from them and your luck will change for the better
- If the psychic medium is too vague with the information
- Inaccurate information (things that you know for a fact is 100% inaccurate on all levels, and cannot even be related to you symbolically) given during the session

The biggest thing to look for is ethics. What are their personal & professional ethics pertaining to them as a psychic/psychic medium?

Ethics & Psychics go hand in hand. There is no way around it. As a psychic/psychic medium, you are expected to be honest, communicate and validate. As a client of a psychic, you are expected to also validate, communicate and be honest. It really is a two-way street.

It (the private or gallery session) can be a loving and heartfelt experience for all accounts.

The problem however comes into when a psychic/psychic medium goes in for shock value, while allowing their ego's take over for their 15-minute of fame.

■ ■

Case example:

A mother makes an appointment with a local psychic to help find her missing child. The child had been missing for several weeks, with the police being unable to find much of a solution.

The reading went as this:

Mother: I need of help. Please help me find my daughter. She is seventeen and missing now for several weeks.
Psychic: Ok, let me take her picture and focus on it (becomes quiet)
Psychic: I see her. She comes to me. She's dead.
Mother: Oh my god! How did she die?
Psychic: She was involved with a drug deal and it went bad. They shot

her twice in the back of the head, then turned five dogs that they had starved for several days to eat her body and the evidence (hands the picture back to the mother). I'm sorry, there is nothing more I can do at this point. She is dead and the evidence is no longer around.

Mother (sobbing): Oh my god! Can you tell me who did this to my daughter? Did she suffer? Where did this happen?

Psychic: No I cannot tell you anything else. I can only see what she shows me.

Mother: How much do I owe you?

Psychic: Nothing. I work for God. I spread his word.

■■

The delivery of this session was no doubt brutal, disturbing and offensive. Whether the psychic/psychic medium saw what they claimed to have seen or not, the delivery of the session was grossly unethical on all levels.

It has been long understood, that when a psychic/psychic medium is working with Law Enforcement on a case, they need to be direct and clear with what they see and hear, whereas when it comes to the parents/surviving family members, or just people in general, their approach during a session should be tempered and free from grandstanding, ego, and non-offensive.

Words have power, especially when it comes from someone who is a psychic/psychic medium.

Ethically, our words as psychic/psychic medium should be above reproach and scrutiny. It is vital that tact is not only learned, but used well whenever dealing with a sitter/client. Shock value is neither needed nor desired.

In fact, it is highly frowned upon and considered unethical.

A psychic/psychic mediums reputation will cast a shadow upon themselves, as well as the next twenty psychic/psychic mediums behind them.

Choose your words carefully, deliver your message respectfully and honestly to the best of your ability and always ask yourself "How would I prefer to receive this type of message?"

Keep in mind that ethically, we are what we say..

RULES FOR PSYCHICS & PSYCHIC MEDIUMS

Newbies to the psychic & the psychic mediumship arena's, are most often bombarded with rules that dictate the 5 "W's", the 2 dreaded "H's" and finally the single "S". For those who are not familiar with the W's & H & S, they are as follows:
- Who (who is the spirit? Who are they with? Who do they belong to?)
- What do they want to say?
- Where are they from? (Are they from a dark place? A good place?
- Why did they choose me to communicate through?
- When should I deliver the message?
- HOW should I interpret the message?
- HOW do I deliver the message?
- SHOULD I help them move on?

So they hit the books and research everything they can, take any course/retreat they can, often they watch every show possible on these topics and closely study each celebrity psychic that comes across their media outlets (social media: Facebook (they join groups), Twitter, Google Plus, YouTube, Etc.), and read THEIR books as well.

What ends up happening more often than not, is that confusion begins to set in and even more questions on top of their confused questions surface, leaving them to feel frustrated and contemplating about giving up and walking away from it all.

Bottom line is that everybody has rules about how to play a game where there is ONLY one true rule:
- THERE ARE NO HARD & FAST RULES

When it comes to opening up the communication with a spirit, talk to your guides first, let them assist you with the communication. Learn to trust your gut.

Once you begin to incorporate your guides, they will assist you in knowing all the W's, all the H's and the S. This is the sole duty of your guides. To assist you.

Another topic that seems to confused many newbie's (also some well-seasoned psychics and psychic mediums) is

SYMBOL INTERPRETATION, DREAM INTERPRETATION & COLOR INTERPRETATION in the following areas:
- Auras
- Dreams
- Psychic Visions
- Spirit communication
- Animal Spirit communication
- Tarot/Crystal Readings

There will never be a "one size fits all" answer to ANY of these. Ever.

It is strictly up for individual interpretation; between the readers gut instinct and their guides.

Yes, there are some good examples which a psychic or a psychic medium can gauge their interpretation on, but they must first ask themselves if it truly fits the situation (session/dream/vision/etc.). This is where their guides and their gut instincts come into play. What fits one situation might not fit the next one.

Case example:

Several years ago, I went to a psychic fair and paid to get my aura read. He saw the following colors in my aura:
- Purple
- Red
- Green

He proceeded to tell me that I had severe anger issues related to my spiritual side and that it was interfering with my psychic side, etc. When I asked him how he came to this fact, he explained that the color red means anger, rage and blood, and repeated that because of my anger issues, it was interfering with my psychic side and my spiritual side.

I explained to him that I loved the color red and have numerous items in my home with the color red, which he went one to explain to me that I only thought I loved it, but in reality I was just angry and raging inside and for me to remove the red items from my home.

I actually left the psychic fair feeling a bit angry that day. I felt strongly that he did not know what he was talking about and I was annoyed that I had wasted money on him (yes, red has many different meanings, not just one).

It wasn't long after that, that I got my aura read again, but this time by someone else. The same colors appeared. I braced myself for another round of "Oh you are filled with rage, etc.", but instead got a pleasant surprised.

What they told me was that I was highly spiritual and had a passion for my spirituality and would end up teaching about spirituality. When I stated that I had many things in my house that were red, because I was fond of the color, they smiled and replied that red is a strong color for strong people.

I left feeling more positive about my session with that reader, than instead with the first reader. Simply because it felt more honest and true to whom I was, and that was something my guides had been telling me all along. Trust your gut.

See the difference in the interpretation of auras, colors and meanings?

When it comes to dreams and visions, the same can also be applied. Just like being a psychic and/or a psychic medium, there is only one true rule:
• There are no rules/there is no "one size fits all"

Simply put, you must learn how to trust your gut instincts and your guides. While it is perfectly OK to learn from others teachings, etc. it will ultimately fall upon you to properly read the messages in which you are given from those who have crossed over.

To bring this home even more, there are over a dozen different meanings/interpretations for a rose, but the only one that truly matters is how your guides and you interpret it during a session or in a dream.

Whenever you get a symbol in a dream or in a vision or even in a session, stop and ask yourself "What does this mean to me and to my client? What do my guides say this means to them?"

There are no hard fast rules in the psychic and psychic mediumship arena. Trust your gut. Trust your guides.

3 MEDITATION, MEDITATION, MEDITATION

RELIGIOUS VS. MEDIUMSHIP

When it comes to mediumship, there is no set structure as to how a psychic medium should conduct their session(s).

There are however, some clear individual practices that have turned into standard dogmas when it comes to practicing mediumship. These practices though, are not followed by everyone and those who are new to mediumship are often confused as to what they should or shouldn't do.

When this confusion takes place, more often than not, the person new to their skills is left wondering if they were meant to be a medium or not. Self-doubt is always counter-productive and rarely gives the person a success story (this is true in any and all areas of life).

Some of the dogma practices concerning mediumship include:
- Meditating daily for at least an hour
- Being a vegetarian/vegan
- Abstaining from alcohol
- Praying
- Connecting with the Holy Spirit first, before speaking with those who have passed
- Following an organized religion
- Using Rosary Beads during prayers
- Only calling upon Angels & God for guidance
- Only reading in circles
- Using new age phrases and words such as "Namaste", "Love & Light", "Bright Blessings", "Go with God", etc.

Now to be clear here, all of the above practices are beautiful in their own right. However, not everyone follows every single one or any at all. Some do, others do not.

Meditation is a powerful tool. It assists in you connecting with your guides and higher self. It should be practiced when you are free of distractions and are well rested (attempting to meditate while you are tired will most likely result in you falling to sleep, thus voiding the meditation itself).

Some people meditate for a few moments a day, others meditate weekly, or whenever they get the chance. The style in which one meditates is also left up to the individual as well (some elect soft music and incense with candles, while others enjoy the quietness of the outdoors, and then there are those who incorporate their own style of music and settings).

Eating habits of psychic mediums is also varied and left up to the person themselves. Some believe that a strict vegan/vegetarian diet is vital to connect with their spiritual paths, while some shove down some of the unhealthiest diets known to mankind. Both still make that connection however.

The same can be said for alcohol consumption. The one rule about alcohol consumption though is to never be under the influence of alcohol while giving readings. This is because alcohol is a mind altering liquid, that renders the person to have a slower thought process, as well as being unable to articulate directions effectively.

To lay it out plainly, if you have consumed even a few glasses of wine, then attempt to read, you most likely will not be able to understand the messages from your guides and/or those from those, who have crossed over.

Praying is always a sensitive topic for many. Many see it as a structured faith based act. For those whom chose to pray, it is both rewarding and quite therapeutic. It helps them connect with their religious/spiritual beliefs. Everyone prays at some point in their lives. Whether it is in an emergency situation or at their dinner table, surrounded by friends and family.

Everyone says a prayer in one fashion or another (pro football players use prayer prior to game time, numerous rock/music stars & bands say prayers prior to concerts, etc.). It is a way of giving thanks for what you have and asking for protection and blessings in the future.

The question comes in here as to whether psychic mediums should pray for guidance and protection before, during and after a reading session(s) or if at all?

Famous Psychic Medium, John Edwards prays with his Rosary before each session, he asks for divine guidance when delivering his messages from the other side.

Some new comer to their gifts might as "Should I as well?" The answer is simple. If prayer is a part of your regular life and something that you do on a daily basis then yes. Without a second thought. Simply yes. This is part of you. By no means should it be left out or left aside.

But if praying regularly is not something that you do often, then why try to do something that might feel "foreign" to your nature? Sure, yes, you can try it and if it feels good then continue.

But if you have to force it and keep reminding yourself to do it, OR you don't get those warm fuzzies from it, then take a step back and ask yourself if you are attempting to use prayers because "everyone else says do it this way". The answer is there inside of you.

Connecting with Higher Spirit first, following an organized religion, praying with a Rosary, calling upon Angels & God for guidance are under the same guidelines as with prayers. If it works for you and this is something that you have done all along, then hey keep at it.

However, same rule of thought, if none of these are your norm, but you wish to try them out, then go for it and see how it feels. But if it doesn't work for you, then don't beat yourself up and think you can't be a psychic medium.

Remember, being a psychic medium is about connecting with those who have crossed over. YES, your heart & spirit needs to be clean here on this subject. Your gift comes from a good place. Listen to your guides (whether they are angels, ancestors, etc.).

Reading in circles has always been a strange concept to some people. Some psychic mediums will only conduct reading sessions within a protected circle of light. This is for them to feel safe to receive and translate messages from those who have crossed over to those who are living. The protective circle is mostly about ensuring that the spirits who come forth are in Gods light and not dark basically.

The last part is about "New Age" sayings "Namaste", "Bright blessings", "Love & Light", Go with God", etc. Many Hindus use the word "Namaste" as a greeting. It is often used to show respect as well to the other person or people, whom you are meeting or departing from.

"Bright Blessings", "love & light" are enduring phrases coming from Pagans, meaning to wish well, without harm, etc. "Go with God" has been used as well as "Go with your goddess".

All of these are simple blessings to wish the traveler well on their journeys, and that no harm comes to them basically. They are beautiful sayings and come from the most purist of many hearts.

In our society, not many people actually run around the streets saying this out loud (when was the last time you heard the bank teller tell you "Here is your money, bright blessings!"), HOWEVER, in certain circles and gatherings it is normal to hear this type of greeting.

Should you say it to your clients at the end of a reading session? Depends, do you ALWAYS talk like this? If you do, then continue. If you do not then don't.

Bottom line, giving reading sessions should never, ever, ever come off as hokey, fake, or superficial. The communication between those who have crossed over to you, and you to your client should flow as easily as you are reading these words right here.

If it feels natural and flows easily as if you are having a normal conversation, then continue. But if at any point you are trying to incorporate something because you think is the "standard norm because everyone else says you have to do it this way" and you just can't relax during the session WITHOUT having to remind yourself "I need to pray", "Don't forget to say Bright blessings", etc. then don't force it on yourself.

Be the psychic medium that you were meant to be, not a carbon copy of 10,000 other store front psychic mediums who might scream out "Love & Light!" as they scam a dollar from someone who thinks Satan is after them.

****PERSONAL NOTE HERE****

I have been a psychic medium basically for all of my life. I've communicated with those who have crossed over since I was a child, and as I grew, so did my gifts.

I love to mediate and try to meditate when I can. However it isn't always often or regular. Nor do I always use incense and candles and new age music. I love to blast my music on anything from Frank Sinatra to Enemin. I find that I can often meditate better during a few tracks of Enemin at times LOL!

Meditation is all about finding your center and grounding yourself. Connecting to your higher self and to your guides.

I am 100% meat lover, junk food craver, etc. But that doesn't mean that I do not try to keep a healthy diet. I do watch my food and try to adhere to a semi healthy level of foods. But there is no way in this universe that I could ever be a vegan or a vegetarian. That isn't going to happen. Just trust me on this.

When it comes to religion, I consider myself to be spiritual but not religious. I feel structured religion is good for some and they are beautiful in nature, but not my cup of tea nor is it something I am interested in.

Not to say I won't visit a church, I have gone in many and love the look, the sense of peacefulness, etc.

I do believe in a higher power and I talk with my guides. My guides are with me 24/7 (as are many of those who have crossed over sometimes LOL). I talk to my guides as if they are people in front of me. Friends.

On the topic of saying "bright blessings", "Love & Light", etc. a few years ago I did try to incorporate those sayings into my verbiage with my clients. They did not feel normal to me at all.

I stumbled over them quite often and many times I would have to remind myself to say "Love & light". Many of my clients looked at me as if I had experienced a stroke. So after a few attempts I dumped them and resumed my normal, everyday language LOL!

Being a psychic medium is a beautiful gift. Whether you believe it comes from God or from the stranger down the road…it is simply a beautiful gift.

It is your gift to explore, expand and to share.

Make the most out of it. Be natural with it. Let it flow as easily as you are reading these words…

That is how true gifts are nurtured.

TRADITIONAL MEDITATION VS. YOUR OWN PREFERENCE

If you were to envision someone meditating, how would you envision them? Wearing loose, white clothing, sitting cross-legged on the floor, maybe in a lotus position, the smell of incense thick in the air, while some new aged music by Yanni plays?

Meditation is when you condition your mind to a certain level of higher consciousness. You become intensely focused at a higher vibrational level. When you achieve this vibrational level, the world around you falls away the instant you become connected with your point of focus.

Meditation is not only practiced in many different paths and ways, but has proven health benefits on the mind and body. It can help lower blood pressure, anxiety, depression, provides a stronger clarity of mind, gives the body more energy, etc.

There are many methods to meditate. Five of the most common are as follows:
- Silence
- Chants
- Mantras/prayers
- Dance/body movement
- Music

Meditation and trance have similar qualities and traits. Both are capable of carrying the human mind to a higher vibration level, thus opening the mind up the receiving messages from other realms, etc.

Silent meditation is perhaps one of the most calm & serene of all mediations. This is where everything around you is still and silent. There is no electrical disturbances and/or humming from electronics, no phone, no noise on any level (not even birds chirping from outside). Some people elect to utilize sound removal headphones to assist in this meditation style.

Meditation with chants/mantras/prayers can be performed with beads (prayer beads, rosary beads, etc.). These chants/mantras/prayers are usually personal and hold significant meaning to the person saying them.

Dance/body movement is also an excellent tool for meditation. Once the body begins to feel the rhythm from a certain beat or sound, it instinctively reacts. Your toes start wiggling, your feet & hands start tapping with the beat, your shoulders start moving, basically your whole body becomes involved. This is our body way of telling you that it is starting to join your mind in the meditation.

Even if dancing is not involved, once your mind focuses on one specific tasks, the body becomes fully engaged at it's highest level. This is also called "getting in the zone". Many artists do this, when they are creating their masterpiece.

Music is the last but certainly not the least method for meditation. Music crosses all culture & language barriers. The beat of a drum (or drums), the strum of a guitar, the keys on a piano, the sound from a saxophone, the voice from a singer, etc. all have a strong potential to initiate a meditative state of mind.

The U.S. military uses Cadence as a form of running/marching for their soldiers. This is a form of group chanting/meditation for the unit. They repeat certain songs/chants/words in unison. It brings them together as one uniform conscious level.

Prisoners on a road crew have been known to sing road work prison songs in unison, during their work. This (like the military running/marching with their cadence), not only assist in a higher productive work flow, but assist in mediation itself. It is a form of meditation.

When it comes to meditating, find which style works best for you. Be aware that your style may change in accordance to your frame of mind. Do not be concerned if traditional methods and songs work for you. The point of meditation is for you to achieve your highest vibrational level.

Once you achieve this level, your third eye becomes engaged at it's fullest, thus opening your psyche up.

On a personal note here

When it comes to me meditating. Many of the traditional ways don't work well with me. In fact, several of the traditional mediation music can actually put me to sleep quicker than a sedative.

I had to learn how to meditate differently.

I find that I can slip into a deep mediation mode when I am shooting (photography) with a model, or out in the wilderness. I instantly focus my energy into one subject and before I know it, everything around me simply falls away. My whole mind & body becomes involved within that focus.

Sometimes I will use something like a virtual fireplace on my kindle as a focus point for my meditation.

Now when I am in the mood to meditate to music, I tend to listen to a variety of artist from Stevie Nicks to Drowning Pool (and everything in between).

Once I focus on the music, the beat, the rhythm, the sound of the singers voice, etc. It all encloses around me. This aides in my mind & body to achieve its high vibrational level.

Same with dancing. I don't dance well. BUT...I dance. My body moves. I get lost in the music, lyrics (chanting/mantras/prayers) with dance. My whole body & mind are instantly connected as one, my third eye soon opens and (again) a higher vibrational level is achieved. This is a form of meditation.

Bottom line, don't think that there is only one way of meditation. The key to meditation is how you create it and use it to achieve your highest vibrational level.

UNEXPECTED TRANCES (what are they & how to deal with them)

A trance is an altered state of half-consciousness. This altered state can be triggered by external stimuli (music, energy, people, places, energy, etc.)

There are basically 3 levels of trance:
• Light
• Full
• Heavy/Deep

Trances can be induced or appear unexpectedly with little to no control over it.

For psychics & psychics mediums, this can feel like a whirlwind of "OMG's", mixed with "WTH (what the hell)", as your mind tries to make sense of the mass amount of information that is rolling over you like a raging Tsunami wave (even the most experienced psychics and psychic mediums have this here and there within their journeys).

A "light trance" is usually soft and gentle like a daydream. It is soothing, comforting, peaceful. Your mind and body feel as if you are being comforted by "warm fuzzies". Many experience this level during Reiki, Yoga or meditation.

A "Full Trance" is heavier. Your body feels heavy, you get somewhat dizzy, sleepy, as if you are being sedated or hypnotized. Images from your mind's eye can begin to appear, your breathing is somewhat labored. Also any sharp (unexpected) sounds can jolt you and feel as if they are slicing through your body.

A "Heavy/Deep" trance is the deepest of all trances. You feel completely submerged in a sea of visions, sounds, & sensations. Your outside body becomes heavy, as if you are being held down and simply cannot move, while your body on the inside feels as if jolts of electricity is being run through your organs (your heart beats wildly sometimes, your stomach might flip flop, etc.).

During this stage, your breathing is very labored (some might feel a ringing/tingling in their ears/head), your mind is very focused. At this state, while you are very much aware of the moment, you, might not remember very much of the details afterwards).

For psychic mediums, an unexpected trance usually comes in at the full to heavy/deep trance stage. The mass amount of images, mixed with swirls of information can actually feel as if you are in a vortex of swirling energies. Your mouth speaks words, relaying information, but it sounds as if you are outside of your own mind and body, etc.

While this state might feel as if it lasts for extended periods of time (some may feel as if it lasts hour or more), it reality it can last several minutes (there is some speculation that time doesn't exist in this level of altered state of consciousness).

When this happens unexpectedly, it is recommended to accept it, allow it to flow through you (as long as you are in a safe place, if you are driving please do NOT engage in this, find a safe place to pull off and allow it to continue OR find the strength to push it down until you can better receive the trance information).

Afterwards, you can feel an array of emotions and body aches, such as:
- Shortness of breath
- Sweaty/shaky hand and/or palms
- Exhaustion (both mental & physical)
- Sleepy/tired
- "Spent"
- Mild to dull headache
- Muscle ache
- Mild disorientation
- Thirsty

It is always recommended to keep 2 things nearby while in a trance state, as well as coming out of a trance state:
- Digital recorder
- Glass of water (some may opt for wine)

The digital recorder is handy to record your words while in trance, while the glass of water (or wine) helps ground and center you upon exiting the trance.

As a last step upon exiting the trance, it is recommended to get a cool refreshing shower, while imaging rays of soft, golden light flowing over your body, helping it to center, ground and heal (during this stage some may opt to also include a sprig or two of Eucalyptus to their showerhead and allow the water to flow over it and onto the body as well).

Afterwards it is recommended that you eat a small (light) meal (and attempt to get a decent night sleep or a catnap if possible), to assist in rebuilding your energy.

NOTICE If symptoms persist then consider seeking medical advice and/or attention promptly

4 SHIELDING

SHIELDING VS. NOT SHIELDING & THE PUBLIC

While it is true that psychics and psychic mediums tend to feel the world around them through energy, those who are Empaths have it much harder, because they feel it on a much deeper and often profound level. There is a constant feedback of data being transferred with the energies.

When a psychic/psychic medium and/or an Empath fails to shield themselves from this constant flow of data, they begin to feel what is best known as "Sensory overload" (too much date being received through energies, causing varies levels of emotional, mental and physical exhaustion.
‘
Symptoms of "Sensory Overload" may appear as:
- Headache (mild to migraine level)
- Body & muscle aches (similar to flu symptoms)
- Exhaustion (feeling drained and unable to function on a daily level)
- Unable to focus (mental exhaustion)
- Emotional Numbness (feeling "blah")

Some of the most common public areas where sensory overload are most often experienced are as follows:
- Thrift/Antique shops
- Flea Markets
- Crowded City Streets
- Traffic Jams

It is vital that proper shielding techniques are not only developed and learned, but created whenever a psychic, psychic medium and/or an

Empath is in the public eye.

There are various levels of shielding:
• Basic shielding (simple shielding when running day to day errands in the public eye)
• Medium shielding (shielding when out in semi crowded public areas such as restaurants, movies, etc.)
• Heavy shielding (shielding when in highly charged public areas, antique shops, traffic jams, crowded city streets, flea markets, etc.)

There are various techniques for shielding and each person must figure out what works best for them. However many new psychics/psychic mediums and/or Empaths are not familiar with how to create a shield.

This is one technique for a basic shield:
• Freshen your body
• Put on fresh clothing
• Ground & center yourself
• Envision yourself in a bubble of white light that goes from your head to your toes
• Feel the warmth from the white light cover you like a blanket
• Seal it with a request/prayer from your spirit guides to help block unwanted energies

This is one technique for a medium shield:
• Freshen your body
• Put on fresh clothing
• Ground & center yourself
• Envision yourself in a bubble of soft blue light that surrounds your entire body
• Feel the energy from the blue light lock your energies to your body, blocking the outside energies
• Seal it with a request/prayer from your spirit guides to help null energies while you are in highly charged emotional public areas

This is one technique for a heavy shield:
• Freshen your body
• Ground & center yourself
• Envision walking onto an "x" spot on the floor, as thick 2-way mirror walls sweep up around you, blocking and instantly deflecting outside energies. Rendering you able to see out, but nothing can be transferred back to you
• Seal it with a request/prayer from your spirit guides to stand guard in

each direction (north, south, east & west) until you deemed otherwise.

Upon returning home from your day in public, it is highly recommended that once you remove your shield, you also get a soothing a shower and change into fresh/clean clothing and eat something light.

OUTSIDE ENERGIES VS. YOUR INSIDE HEALTH

We are surrounded by a buffet table of energies throughout the day and night. Energy comes in all forms and styles:
- People
- Events & Situations
- Emotions
- Non-living items such as T.V.'s, fans, computers, etc. (basically anything electrical),
- Animals
- Nature itself
- Buildings, etc.

If you were to place everything into two basic groups, the groups would look like this:
- Natural
- Man-made

Babies and young children are often prone to become upset and "off balanced" when they are overly stimulated in a situation (be it if their parents are fighting, or anywhere where there is an overload of confusion ad chattering/activity going on around basically).

When this happens (if the parent(s) recognizes this for what it is), the parent removes the child to a quiet area so that they may calm down and center themselves again (in other words, the child has the quietness they need to calm themselves down, while also having the security of a trust parent to help them calm down).

This results in the child/baby calming down and feeling balanced enough to once again return to the situation or to become involved with another situation, where they are able to function in a better capacity (with less stimulation and chaos).

We as Psychics, Psychic Mediums and especially those of us who are Empaths, also fall prey to this actually quite often.

Natural energies primarily come from nature and animals themselves (with the exception of crystals, polished crystals still have the same energies as raw crystals). When your mind and body connects with them, you tend to feel more at peace, your body reacts in a positive manner, you seem to feel more "alive" with energy.

Overall, you react with a stronger, happier and more balanced sense about you.

Man-Made energies tend to have very conflicted variations of energies, almost to the point of chaos.

When a psychic or a psychic medium gets around too much of these man-made energies, it begins to have an effect on your mind, body, and spirit (especially if you are an Empath).

How can you recognize what is going on? Simple look for these signals:
• You start to feel confused (slightly at first, then increases), unable to effectively concentrate
• You feel as if you are being pulled in to many different directions
• You feel as if you are over-whelmed and tired/lethargic
• Physically, you feel as if you are out of shape (or have some sort of a chest cold/infection that is possibly building in your lungs), you feel congested, etc.
• You start to get easily annoyed when around a lot of electrical appliances (hearing their humming, feeling a fan directly on you, even the constant chime from your cell phone, etc.)
• You feel the urge to unplug/shut off all electrical items around you for some peace and quiet, or to sleep

Case example:

Not too long ago, I went to my family doctor, certain that something was wrong with me. I had been unable to walk around a small block with my husband and dog, without having to stop to catch my breath, etc.

Quite frankly it was starting to scare the hell out of me because I always took pride in knowing my body and this was something I just could not fix on my own.

He checked me out and gave me a clean bill of health and explained that it could be the fact that I have gained a few pounds and that my body just is not used to that extra weight (he said this as the coward backed up LOL!)

and that the coral dust in the air from all of the recent sewer pipe installments mixed in could possibly be what's going on.

So I left his office, a few less dollars in my bank account and plotting out a new diet/exercise plan.

Short time later, I was STILL experiencing a hard time walking a small block. In fact it had gotten to the point where I hated to be outside. I hated walking my dog, I simply could not breathe, or walk a lot.

So the other day, my hubby takes me on a surprised picnic out on No Name Key (VERY quiet, NO powerlines, NOTHING except ocean, trails, wildlife, etc. and the houses are all run by solar energy). After the picnic we walked on one of the many paths, back in the woods.

As we returned back to the car, he pointed out that we had walked a total of 5 miles and I kept up with him at a road march pace (army road march meaning a fast, consistent style of walk), while carrying one a lively conversation, with only having to stop once and that was to grab a few sips of water. Even upon us returning home, I felt energized and relaxed.

I was confused and wanted to see what this was about. So I did an experiment. The next day, we walked around the block with our dog. True to form, I had to stop several times to catch my breath and was actually starting to get annoyed (forget talking).

THEN we drove out to a different natural area (a place I often do photo shoots in), it has a steep hill to walk up and down, in order to get to the water. I did it with NO issue what so ever, then we drove back to No Name Key and we walked around there again for another 3 miles or so.

The next day we walked around the block again, only this time I noticed the energies from the sewer lines that were laying out, ready to be planted in the ground, I focused on the machines and equipment that were lingering out as well, the houses were all busy with humming's, people fighting, laughing, music, busy cars and bikes zipping by us, etc.

It was 100% pure chaos. It was so thick that I couldn't get my breath. I had to stop to catch my breath several times.

I wasn't out of shape (OK maybe yes I did pack on a few extra pounds I won't deny that), my body was reacting to the over stimulated chaotic man-made energies in my area and it was trying to tell me to separate myself from it once in a while, as well as for me to create a different type of shield.

I share my story with you so that you can understand the various forms of energies that are constantly around you 24/7 and how you must learn how to work with them, or shield yourself when you are around them, if you must.

I know now personally, that I am perhaps extra sensitive to external man-made energies (especially if they are all clustered together) and therefore when I am around them I have to incorporate an extra strong shield, so that it doesn't affect my body, as the context as it had been previously.

BTW I did shield myself better the next time I went outside for a small block walk and while it wasn't as perfect as when I am out in the nature itself (barefoot cause I feel the earths energies faster and stronger), it was a better walk overall.

TOP HOTSPOTS WITH COMBUSTIBLE ENERGIES AND WHY YOU SHOULD EXTRA SHIELD YOURSELF FROM THEM

There are a few hotspots that hold combustible energies that can (and often) directly affects psychics/psychic medium and/or Empaths. They are:
- Hospitals
- Police stations/Courtrooms
- Crowded Restaurants
- Crowded Shopping Malls

Combustible energies are pockets of tightly enclosed energies that are contained in one specific area, with no-where else to go.

When a psychic/psychic medium and/or an Empath encounter these areas, they are immediately hit with these energies. Another way to describe this is:

Gas fumes from stove (combustible energies) + cigarette lighter (psychic/psychic medium and/or Empath) = Explosion

Many describe it as being hit in the face hard, while some others describe it as being hit in the stomach hard. Either way, they are hit and it impacts their senses and ability to continue on with whatever they were there to do in the first place.

HOSPITALS are perhaps the biggest places for containing combustible energies. This is because whenever people generally go to the hospital, it is (usually) one of three reasons:
- A birth
- A sickness (operation & chemo included)
- A death

Add in there, grief and concern (or celebrations) from loved ones, along with the personal issues from the medical staff (overworked, tired, hungry, frustrated, still mad from fighting with their partners, or other family based drama, perhaps they themselves are not feeling well, etc.).

Police stations/Courtrooms are also known to have pockets of combustible energies in them, mainly because of the high range of emotions from:
- Those who have been arrested and/or those being accused of a crime and are in trial
- Those filing a police report because a crime has happened to them and/or those in a courtroom against someone who has committed a crime against them or their loved one(s)
- The (overall) chaotic atmosphere stemming from the pressures from the police to solve the cases, the lawyers to win the cases (either side), media with the media personnel hanging around trying to get the "scoop"

Crowded restaurants and shopping malls have their own special blend of combustible energies (especially during the major holidays).

The reasons they made the list in hotspots of combustible energies is because more often than not, there is always an element of pressures stemming from:
- Shops needing to have an increase in sales than the year before
- The retail salesperson having to reach their individual sales/commission goal (along with whatever is going on in their personal life)
- Servers and cooks feel pressure to perform at top level in overly crowded restaurants
- Owners/Managers feel the pressure to maintain a high level of service, while also keeping their meal prices at a reasonable level

Now when you throw in the average consumer who goes into the mall to shop for a holiday gift, then take the family out for a meal afterwards, the following emotions are known to pop up:
- Kids are hungry and tired

- Parents are hungry, tired, distracted and frustrated
- Non-children adults, who go out to shop and a meal are distracted by the chaotic energies from the parents with children

Effective and extra shielding is not only warranted, but vital, when entering these types of environments.

One such method is known as a "Golden Shield". This golden shield actually surrounds you in a warm golden light, keeping you calm and level headed, able to go about and enjoy your events and outings, with little to no outside interference from surrounding combustible energies.

To make the "Golden Shield":
- Envision a large golden orb appearing in front of you
- Step into that large orb, feeling it surround you like a cocoon
- Allow yourself to soak in its warmth
- Request the assistance from your guides to walk along side of you, blocking others from entering your "Golden Shield"

Once you are home, visualize stepping out of the "Golden Shield", then ask your guides to remove it, while you go take a warm shower and change your clothes.

5 MANIFESTING YOUR ABILITIES

SPIRITUAL AWAKENING

A spiritual awakening can occur at different stages during a person's life. Sometimes it can occur during traumatic events/tragedies, psychical and/or psychological changes (being gravely ill for a long period of time, hormonal changes such as starting a menstrual cycle, menopause, pregnancy, etc.), NDE (near death experience), etc.

When a person does experience an awakening, it can jolt the mind/body/spirit into a panic stage. This is often due to the heightened stages of each of our 5 senses (sight/sense/smell/taste/touch) that are activated during such events/experiences.

Some of the signs are a spiritual awakening are:
- Increased activity of psychic abilities, as well as other paranormal experiences (vivid dreams, out of body experiences, astral traveling, etc.)
- Sensitivity to negative energies (whether in people, locations, objects, etc.)
- Change in sleeping/eating habits (irregular sleep patterns, sleeping for a few hours then able to function all day without being tired, extreme thirst, cravings for certain foods, etc.)
- Changes in interpersonal relationships with family/friends (being unable to be around certain ones suddenly, etc.)
- Instinctive primal behaviors (nesting/clearing out junk, desire to "return" back to basic way of life, sexual appetite changes/increases, etc.)
- Unexplained panic attacks (with no logical explanation, etc.)
- Psychical aches/pains (cramps, headaches, neck/shoulder ache, dizziness/vertigo, stomach/digestive issues, etc.)
- Heightened sensitivity to fabrics (your skin's reaction to fabric in

general: Suddenly being unable to wear something due to how it "feels" on your body, or desiring to have a certain fabric on your body because it "soothes" you, etc.)
- Change in your hobbies/interests
- Overwhelming feelings of being connected to the energies of the world around you

When you feel these changes start to take place, it is normal to fear it, to question it, to question yourself and your level of sanity.

It is important that you not fight against these changed, but rather embrace and learn how to work with them as they occur. Let them flow as they occur within & around you.

Adapting to the changes will be beneficial while on your spirituality journey.

"There are no constraints on the human mind, no walls around the human spirit, no barriers to our progress except those we ourselves erect." - Ronald Reagan.

INSTANT SOUP DOES NOT MEAN INSTANT SPIRITUALITY

Just add water, stir and heat and BOOM! You got instant soup in less than 2 minutes! Too bad everything in life can't be that quick for good results right? Or no?

An instant result does not always mean worthwhile results. Sometimes the results you get from instant results often leave you unsatisfied and wondering if maybe you should have had something else instead but it was an overall disappointment in the end.

This is the very same with your spirituality path. If you rush through it, skip over vital pivots or even place yourself on a strict time limit for completion, you will without a doubt miss out on the journey itself.

All spiritual journeys have a very long path that is often filled with twists and turns before achieving their ultimate level. You (as the seeker of your own spiritual wisdom) were created to learn (and enjoy) about your spirituality in the time that was decided prior to your being born into this life.

Each of us learn at different paces, each of us must endure different lessons along the way, lessons that are uniquely to us and our own spiritual paths. There is no rushing. No just add water and boom instant soup. No sense in it. We would not learn nor remember anything that way.

Some of us start early in childhood, but lack of understanding, while others start later in life and feel that we are running out of time so we lack the patience.

While this is normal for us to feel this as humans, it is also self-defeating and more often than not, some elect to give up far too soon, before the real knowledge and experiences unfold before their eyes.

So ask yourself tonight as you lay down to sleep. Ask yourself "Do I want instant soup or do I want to experience my true spiritual journey and learn?

MANIFESTING YOUR PSYCHIC ABILITIES

Everyone has psychic abilities. Before we were born, we possessed the capabilities to communicate with other entities and spirits. Basically our abilities have been with us since our souls were formed.

When we were young, we were not told that seeing or feeling "something/someone" is not normal. But as we grew up, society and family dynamics began to dictate as to how we should view the world and ourselves.

During this period, we (some of us) were told that psychic abilities, etc. does not exist, or is bad and that we should fear it or risk being consumed by evil.

When this happens, an "awakening" can occur (most often during the onset of a traumatic event, etc.) and we then become aware of "something" within us, always present, just under the surface (like an itch in the middle of your back that you just can't get too).

We are then left with a barrage of questions and little to no true answers. So what do we do? Where can we turn?

Many elect to seek out answers anywhere they can: internet, metaphysical stores, churches, books, videos, etc.

While these resources are most often extremely useful, there is a saying that still holds true:
"What you seek outward must first be sought inward"

In order for us to manifest our abilities, we must first connect within us.

In order to do this, we must first be able to go beyond mediation. We must tap into our "core self" and feel it our own unique energy flow. Each person has two energy sources (inward and outward).

In order to do this, we must forget the standard six senses:
- Sigh
- Smell
- Taste
- Hear
- Sense
- Touch

Instead of using those senses, we must simply go inward ourselves (our bodies) and exist.

Try this brief exercise (10 minutes is recommended):
- Get comfortable as if starting to mediate
- Close your eyes/clear your mind
- Go inward and exist

Don't think about anything, merely "exist" within your body. Focus on each part of your body from the inside. Soon you should begin to feel as if an electrical current is flowing up and down your body, tingling, pulsating (sometimes strong, sometimes ever so slightly).

Once you feel begin to feel this current, keep with it, go along with it as it moves throughout your body. What this is is your body sending and receiving energy transmissions.

Afterwards, open your eyes and simply "exist" once more. No thought patterns, no movement (no eye movement, etc.), nothing but allowing the energy transmissions to continue through you, only this time with your eyes open (basically as if you are in a mist of suspended animation).

After a few moments, blink several times, yawn, get up and stretch (move your neck, shoulders, back, legs, hips, wiggle your toes, etc.). Allow your mind to process what just happened.

Don't question what happened, don't attempt to analyze what happened, but allow your mind to process what happened.

Try to do this daily for a full week (7 days).

After a week, not only should you begin to notice you a stronger connection to your abilities, but your six basic senses should also be attuned to higher levels (some even notice that their foods taste different on several levels because of both their smell and taste buds are heightened and have become more sensitive, while some comment that their sinuses & lungs "feel" more open and less cluttered with debris).

Next, you need to build a connection between that energy flow and your meditation. The way to do this is by visualization technique:
- Prior to you getting ready to enter our meditative state, go inward and allow yourself to exist
- Once you feel the energy surge flowing throughout your body, visualize your body as an energy circuit board, connecting the wires in a certain fashion, so the energy flows easier, smoother and faster
- Allow yourself to pause for a few moments so that the flow increases in strength (you should begin to feel a pulsation sensation at this point within your body)
- Enter your meditative state now, allowing the energy surge to blend with your meditation. Taking you deeper and deeper
- Visualize yourself walking through a field of flowers, with each step, the energy exchange between the flowers and you enhances the vibrancy and aroma of the flowers, surrounding you and the flowers in a halo of vibrant colors
- Once you reach the middle of the field of flowers, lay down and look up
- Visualize the halo of vibrant colors forming a dome above you and the flowers, enclosing you, as the aroma from the flowers fills your body with each inhale you take
- Stay there and allow the energy flow to increase within the dome, until the vibration is pulsating within your ears
- Get up and start to walk back away from the field of flowers, with each step, the dome slowly fades away, clearing away to clear, bright skies
- Once you are completely away from the field of flowers, turn to look back at it, you will notice that the dome of vibrant colors has turned into soft sparkly glitter in the sky
- Open your eyes, allow yourself to exist for a few extra moments, soaking in your meditation, giving your inner energy flow time to simmer

down and return to normal
- Stand up, stretch your body and muscles (especially your hands/fingers & feet/toes)

Try to do this type of meditation for another 7 days. Again, be sure not to analyze or label anything, just let it exist. Let you exist. No labels or analyzing are needed.

The last part of this manifesting is to connect your inner energy to your abilities. This in the end will connect your inner energy flow to your outer energy flow overall. Overall enhancing all of your abilities, opening you up more.

Below is a small list of abilities, along with a brief description on how to blend your inner energy flow to your outer flow to that ability:
- These techniques are to be performed prior to using your abilities, much like pre work before initializing your abilities

Psychometry (the ability to read objects, gathering & receiving images/information about people/places, etc. associated with that object: clothing, pictures, wallets, cell phones, etc.):
- Close your eyes, go inward to your inner energy core and exist for a few moments quietly
- Feel your energy transmitting stronger and stronger, pulsating throughout your body
- Open your eyes, if you are to hold an object, now is the time to pick it up and hold it in your hands (your hands should be tingling right now), if you are focusing on an image, allow your eyes to lock on the image, while your energy flows to the image (through your eyes)
- Allow the information to flow to you, much like a circuit board of energy, total and complete absorption of information mixed with energies

Reiki (the ability to improving the flow of energy in a person through hands on or hands off techniques):
- Close your eyes and go inward to your energy core and exist for a few moments quietly
- Feel the energy transmitting through your spine, flowing through your hands (some feel their hands become extremely warm to hot during this process)
- While keeping your eyes closed, slowly move your hands just above the person in front of you, allowing your energy to smooth out their wrinkles
- Open your eyes and focus on each spot where you feel a "coolness",

keep rotating your hands there, massaging deep outwardly, breaking up their congestion in that area of their body
- As a last move, begin at the top of their head and while moving slowly down their body, pausing at each Chakara to enhance them, electrifying them (be sure to focus on their third eye, their hands/fingers and the bottoms of their feet because these areas is where majority of their energy flows from these areas and must be restored to full capacity)

Shielding (the ability to protect one's personal space by envisioning an invisible shield of protection):
- Close your eyes and go inward
- Allow your inner energy circuit board activate and become stronger with each breath
- With your hands, allow your energy to flow through your palms, swirling around as you flow over your body
- Then spread your palms outward and place the shield around your personal space area (approximately 1 full arms-length from your body), creating a mobile dorm around you of electric blue energy shield

Mediumship (the communication between the living and those who have crossed over into the afterlife, also communication with entities in the spirit world):
- Close your eyes and go inward to your energy source, feeling it charge up
- Open your eyes when you feel your body vibrating from inside to the outside
- Activate the opening between the spirit world and yourself
- Feel the pulsation grow stronger and stronger
- With each spirit that comes forth, allow your inner energy to fully mesh with theirs, giving way to stronger, more powerful images and messages

Psychic (the ability to read a person, receives images/visions of possible future/past events/encounters, etc.):
- Close your eyes and go inward
- Activate your inner energy source, allowing it to charge up fully
- Once you feel yourself vibrating, open your eyes
- Focus on the person, as if you are looking at a painting, no definitions needed, simply exist while your energies blend with theirs
- Allow their information to flow through your energy, absorb everything

It should be noted here that upon finishing working with your abilities in this style, it is recommended that you close your inner energy source, as well as your outward energy.

To do this you should:
• Close your eyes and go inward, envisioning your energy course slowing down, eventually turning off and cooling down (you should feel your body calming down, as well as a slight cooling sensation throughout your body)
• Open your eyes, exist quietly for an extra moment or two
• Exhale and stretch, while you remove yourself from the activity you were doing

*** At this point is it recommended that you grab a light snack and something cool to drink ***

DEALING WITH THE DARKER SIDE OF READINGS

There comes a point in any and all psychic/psychic mediums paths where they will encounter the reading of a spirit who has crossed over due to unpleasant circumstances (suicide, homicide, etc.).

One of the main triggers to the darker side of readings is when chaos/stress invades your life.

When they become apparent, it can sometimes be so over whelming to where you (the psychic/psychic medium)feel panic-driven, thus wishing to shut down and ignore your abilities all together.

There are 3 unspoken hard fast rules that come along with being a psychic/psychic medium:
• Your guides will continuously light your path, by enhancing your overall growth
• Not every reading will be sprinkled with puppies and rainbows
• Not every psychic/psychic medium can effectively process the darker side of readings

Guides are assigned to us from the moment of our existence, they help use select our parents, childhood, life, etc. in order to learn the lessons that we are designated to learn during this lifetime.

Their sole job is to guide us on our path. This means that they (from time to time) will attempt to engage us with encounters to help us grow spiritualty.

From time to time, we will encounter psychic readings where the situation (whether it is a vivid/astral dream or a reading) is less than pleasant.

In some encounters, the sensations can be so intense (vivid smells, pain, agony, fear, anger, etc.) that it feels as if you can being over-run by them. The best way to address this is by centering and grounding yourself and slowly processing it, with the understanding that you are "seeing" it NOT actually living it (this will take practice)

The final hard fast rule of psychic readings is that not every psychic/psychic medium can handle the dark side. Some prefer to only see "love & light" tones in life.

This is not to say they are not psychics/psychic mediums…but they have placed limits on their abilities by choice. Their choice. And nobody has a right to say whether they are right or wrong with their personal decision.

PERSONAL DISCLOSURE:

I have been subjected to the darker side of spirit encounters since childhood (my first true spirit encounter was that of a murder victim in the home, which I grew up in.

Flash forward to when my husband (boyfriend at the time) was taking me to see his family for the first time, I began to experience vivid and harsh sensations during the trip (my stomach hurt, my ears kept exploding, I kept smelling & tasting metal and kept seeing flashes of red in my eyes.

My husband thought it was a case of nerves and healing from surgery (I just had a hysterectomy and no at that time he was not aware of my being a psychic medium, I was waiting for the right time to tell him, which in the end would come back to bite me on my ass).

We arrived at his sister's house. I took two Tylenols, showered and changed into fresh clothes to go out with my husband and his sister, to meet everyone else. Still my nerves were raw. I couldn't shake it. Every sense in me was on fire and sending me into more chaos alone.

We ended up at a local bar for drinks. I couldn't calm down. In fact, it got worse. I tried dancing, no luck. I tried drinking a drink, nope. Nothing worked.

My husband couldn't understand what the hell was wrong with me and honestly at that point I didn't know either!

He was walking me to the restroom, when his sister came up with another drink, then my husband saw one of his uncles and asked that we stay there, while he went to get him from the bar.

Once his uncle came and shook my hand…everything came into clear and vivid view. I saw the following:
- His uncle getting shot in the stomach
- I felt the bullet hit his stomach (felt like my stomach)
- I saw the blood covering his eyes
- I tasted the blood in his mouth
- I felt my ears explode from the sound of the bullet

My knees felt weak, my husband sister guided me to the bathroom so I could wash my face and regroup.

I went to my husband in ears and begged him for us to leave so I could explain everything to him. After a few moments, he gave in and took me to a quiet diner down the road. There we talked over coffee and pie.

He brushed it off as nerves, etc.

Once we returned to my parent's home, there was a message from his sister on the answering machine.

His uncle had been fatally shot in the bar no more than 5 minutes after we left the bar.

Dealing with the darker side of readings is no puppies and rainbows at all.

Dealing and processing them takes time and a strong soul.

The biggest thing is that you have to understand that while you (the psychic/psychic medium) are going through this…you are a conduit relating the information for a reason (whether to help the police in a case, or to help you grow overall in your abilities, etc.).

AFTER dealing with encounters like this, it is vital that you give yourself some quality down time by pampering yourself, so something completely

opposite from your spirituality, such as:
- Go for a walk/run (physical activity always helps remove the stress)
- Color/draw/paint/etc. (anything artistically related can actually assist in calming you down)
- Dance (same as with any physical activity)
- Singing (you don't have to be good...just sing)

Many of those in stressful and demanding careers (military, firefighting, police, etc.) have taken up side hobby's such as needlepoint, crocheting, etc. to give them that quality downtime so that they can continue with their careers.

BTW my husband who is a sniper in the army and a Federal cop likes to macramé, woodburn and color! Myself, I dance and sing!

6 GUIDES

YOUR GUIDES (TYPES, HOW MANY, ETC.)

Whether or you a psychic medium or just another person on this planet, you have guides around you. You have always had guides around you from the moment you are conceived.

There are several types of guides, some enter our lives for specific time frames, while some stick with us during our entire existence.

Some types of guides are explained below:
• Soul Guides: Some refer to them as "Your inner voice". They are actually part of your soul. Your soul existed before you were born. When it was decided that you would be reborn (in many instances) or simply born into your current existence, part of your soul stayed behind to learn lessons, while "your inner voice" guide tagged along, guiding you, advising you, keep you company, etc. They are most like you, because they are you. They will stick with you during your entire journey.
• Time Guides: These guides will (sometimes) appear themselves to you via other people (stranger in passing who gives you some really good advice when you need it the most, offer you assistance in some way, etc.). They help. That's their sole job. To assist you during a specific period of time. Then once that task is completed, they are gone. But the lesson, assistance, etc. stays with you.
• Ancestral Guides: Ancestral guides are those within your blood line. They could be that great grandmother 3 times removed, whom you have never met before, and/or a recent parent who has passed over, etc. They pop in and out during various periods, to offer guidance as needed. Often they assist in keeping you within the connected with the family ways

(whether you know it or not).

• Animal Guides: Animal guides are perhaps the most special in many instances. These spiritual guides will enter your dreams, they will appear in physical form, etc. When they do, you instantly feel a connection. (Sometimes) that instant connection is so intense, it can bring tears to your eyes. It can be a humbling experience. Their job is to guide by showing you their ways of behavior, how they live, how they interact, etc. They can also deliver messages to you from the other side in your dreams, etc.

***NOTE: It is possible to have a mythological animal as a guide, as well as a real one. Always remember that each one offers guidance in their own style. Also they can come in and out of your life, as well as one or two who stay beside you on your journey.

It is possible to have more than one guide with you (yes it can get a little crowded at times). Communicating with your guides is as simple as clearing your mind and listening to them.

ARE YOU WORKING WITH YOUR TEAM?

Even though this is a very simple question, the answer is not always simple to give. In order for us to have the capability to work with our team, we must first learn who is on our team, as well as their roles and how they interact with us on our paths (personal, professional, spiritual, etc.)

Spiritualty, the word "team" refers to your guides (both spiritual & animal). Their sole role in your life is to provide you with guidance. They do this through several different methods:
• Your dreams (fantasy based/realistic based/etc.)
• Your intuition (gut instincts/little voice inside of you/etc.)
• Symbols (seeing/hearing a repetitive image/number/message/etc.)
• Music (a song that won't leave your mind/lyrics/beat and/or rhythm/etc.)
  • People (strangers/friends/family/etc.)
  • Animals (domestic & wild)
  • Media (social media/television/etc.)
  • Spirits (those who have crossed over/etc.)

Your team will guide and interact with you on everything from the mundane to the most complexed and vital decisions in your life. That is their role.

Your role is to acknowledge and work with them. But how? Here are a few simple ideas to get you started:

• Dream journal: By keeping a dream journal and reviewing it regularly, certain messages will begin to appear, thus assisting you in seeking the answers that you may need for a specific issue. It is important to maintain some level of a dream journal based on the fact that as we (as humans) as sleeping, we become more open to receive messages and information from the other side and from our team (guides). This is also an excellent tool to use for attempting to work out potential issues/problems in your life.

• Listen to your intuition: Pausing long enough to simply listen to what your inner voice/gut/etc. is telling you, enables you to hone in to potential solutions to your inner questions (this goes far beyond the simple "which street should I turn on right now?"). As you pause, take notice to the urgency/persistence & tone of your intuition. Is it soft and subtle? Or is it loud and gnarling in the front part of your brain? Is it persistent? What is it saying exactly? A suggestion would be to sit down (quietly) with a pen and paper to write it (what you are hearing/feeling) out on paper, then review it for a few moments. Ask your team if this is what they are asking/urging? What is their response? Then weigh the pros and cons of each side. How do you feel about each (potential) result? How does your team feel about each (potential) result?

• Symbols: Often, your team will use symbols (in a repetitive style) to get your attention. These symbols can be in the form of anything from a group of numbers, to sound(s), even messages. When these happen, it is urged to stop and make notation of them. Break it down to the basics before trying to understand them. Ask yourself and your team "what is the message here?". Examine it, dissect it. For instance, perhaps you have a meeting with a new client to attend and each time you think of them, you keep seeing the color red. Now the color red has different meanings: Passion/Anger/Love/Lust/Power/Etc., so it is important to evaluate what else is attached to this symbol? Are you also feeling powerful emotions when this symbol appears? Ask your team why are they sending this symbol to you in relation to this client? Is it a warning? Or are they just trying to give you a "heads up" on the client's personality?

• Music is perhaps one of the most common method your team will use to gain your attention. It can be any style of music (even the ones you may not like or have ever listened to before). Your team will send you a song in all forms of your life: sleeping, working on a different task, watching television, hanging out with friends/family, etc. When this happens, stop and listen to the song. If you can, research the lyrics and read them. What do the lyrics say? What do they mean? What about the rhythm? What about the video to the song? What about the singer/band? What role do they play with the message? Ask your guides how does this particular song relate to your present situation? Sometimes a song offers more power and more guidance than you would think.

• People are often sent to us as a message (especially strangers) during difficult moments of our lives. Your team will send them out to deliver a variety of messages from a simple "Your tire looks low" (random person next to you getting gas), to a distant relative calling you up and talking about something from their past that relates to a situation you may be presented with currently, etc. When this happens, it is important that you (once again) pause long enough to thoroughly listen to the message. Sometimes it is a very subtle message, while other times, it is straight in your face.

• Animals being used as messages is always considered special. Why? Because animals have no hidden agendas. When your team sends you an animal as a message, look at the whole message. Break it down: What type of animal is it? What are their traits? Where are you seeing it? In what context are you seeing it? What are your feelings/emotions when you see it? Sometimes your team will send an animal as a warning about a potential issue, whereas other moments, they could send you an animal as a message of hope or determination.

• Media (especially social media) has taken a dominant role in society. So it is not uncommon for your team to send messages this way as well. More often than not, your team will utilize the media, along with other methods (song, symbols, animal, etc.). When this happens, take note and look at everything from all angles. Examine the message thoroughly. Ask your team how does this relate to your life? A good example of this style of message is when you need to make a dentist appointment but have been really busy and have not in the last year or so (for whatever reason). Suddenly, you are seeing commercials for professional teeth whitening or how gum disease play a factor in heart attacks, etc., then as you go outside you come across a dog with some of their teeth missing, etc. It is important to take note of the message here.

• Spirit communication is also another vital method your team uses to send you messages. When this happens, pause and look at the spirit themselves. Do you know them? Did you know them at some point? What are they trying to tell you? Is it an urgent message of "Don't go down that road!" type? Or is it your grandmother showing you her secret ingredient in her spaghetti recipe that could also work in your lasagna recipe as well? Once you factor in everything and compare this to your current situation, you will begin to notice the answer quite clearly.

Establishing a strong working relationship with your team is vital for spiritual development. It is important to always understand the many different roles your team plays in your life.

Once you create that bond of communication, you will begin to notice these messages from your team on a regular basis and once that happens, many of your life questions will become easier to answer.

Remember that there are three key factors here and they are: (1) to listen actively, (2) to evaluate actively and (3) to trust actively.

7 GIVING READINGS

GAUGING SITTERS COMFORT LEVEL DURING READINGS

Whenever you are about to give a reading, it is vital that you gauge the sitters comfort level.

One of the first ways to do this is reading their body language.

When reading their body language you must look for these important key factors:
- Are their hands tightly clasped together? Are the fingers tightly curled up within the hand itself? Are their hands sweaty? Can you see the whites of their knuckles? Are they fiddling with something (ring, watch, etc.?), are they sitting on their hands?
- Are their arms crossed protectively in front of them? Rigid?
- How are their feet? Are they pointed towards you or pointed off to the side or curled around the chair?
- Are they performing self-pacifying movements with their hands (stroking their throat, or their playing with their hair, etc.)?
- How is the tone of their voice? Strained, high pitched, shaky, etc.
- How is their breathing rate? Quick & shallow?
- How is their eye contact with you? Are they making eye contact? Looking away (floor, etc.)?
- Are they nibbling on their lips, picking at a bump/sore, etc.?

If you answered yes to a few of these with the sitter, then proceed with caution. What they are telling you is that while yes they might wish to have a reading, they are simply nervous for any possible number of reasons:
- First time ever having a reading (first few times usually makes for a nervous sitter)
- First time ever receiving a reading from you (comfort level)

- (perhaps) feeling conflicted about receiving a reading and their personal religious and/or family views, etc.
- Not really sure if they are ready to open communication with the other side and what could possibly be said (or revealed) during session.

If your sitter is showing signs of being nervous, take time and talk about it with them. Let them get everything out. Listen. The key word is to listen.

Truly listen. Display a calm body posture (unclasp your hands, lean in, make eye contact, use a soft, even tone in your voice, be engaging during the conversation (nod in acknowledgement), etc.

It is important that you reassure them that they are in control and if they wish to not have a reading at that point that would be ok with you. If they wished to have a reading but certain things are not permitted to be discussed and/or revealed, cover it at that point in time.

If they wish to have everything discussed that would be fine with you as well. Should that happen, understand that tact is still required during the reading.

Some basic guidelines while in session are as follows:
- ANYTHING MEDICAL should always be covered/discussed with a pure "kid glove" tone. At NO point during the session should the reader ever blurt out "Cancer", "AIDS", Etc. If a medical topic comes up (either from the other side or wherever), it is recommended that the reader pause for a few moments, asking for assistance from their guides (higher power, etc.), then check with the sitter to see how they wish to receive this information before proceeding.
- DEATHS is also another sensitive topic (for obvious reasons). Psychic mediums are often privy to graphic details pertaining to the passing of a soul. The other side doesn't have a filter when it comes to this information in many instances, so again check in with your guides and with the sitter before proceeding.
- VIOLENT ACTS is a knee jerking topic to have out during the session. Sensitivity areas such as rape, physical assault, incest, etc. is enough (sometimes) to make even the strongest sitter want to get up and leave the session. Sometimes, our guides show us intimate, personal situations of the sitter. What is advised here when this happens, refer back to gauging the sitters comfort level. Let them take control over the information and how it is delivered and to what extent.

One highly important thing to always remember is:
NOT EVERYONE NEEDS TO KNOW EVERYTHING ALL OF THE TIME

COLD READING/HOT READING VS. REAL READINGS

As you begin your spiritual journey to explore your psychic abilities, etc., you will come across words such as: Cold Reading & Hot Reading.

A Cold Reading is where a psychic knows nothing about the sitter/client they are talking to, and they tend to use a fair amount of generic statements, mixed with questions, and is more often reading facial reactions to their questions and responses. For example:

Psychic: "I'm getting an older woman with arthritis in your family. Do you have a grandmother who had arthritis?"
Sitter: "Yes I do!"
Psychic: "And is she the type of grandmother who enjoyed the family?"
Sitter: "Yes!"
Psychic: "Good and how long has she been dead?"
Sitter: "She isn't. She is still alive."
Psychic: "I see. Then how long have the two of you been distant from each other? I sense a distance between the two of you? Does she live in a group home?"
Sitter: "We're not. I just had lunch with her the other week at her house!"
Psychic: "OK, well know that she loves you and that worries about you."

How many mistakes can you figure out that the psychic made during this session? The psychic went wrong in the following ways:
• Was very generic about the person they "felt" (it is very plausible that many grandmothers have some form of arthritis, as it is also true that most will have an older female in their families, most of whom are grandmothers)
• Asked a lot of questions
• Gave NO solid validation

A Hot Reading is where a psychic has received some background information about the sitter/client and uses it as a basis for their session. For example:

Prior to the session, the psychic uses the sitter's/client name to search on social media (Facebook, twitter, etc.) and finds their profile, email, and mutual friends, etc.

▪▪

Psychic: "Hi Barb! Thank you for coming today!"

Sitter: "Oh I am excited to be here!"

Psychic: "OK so let's get started! I'm getting that you have just broke up with your boyfriend! Now he cheated on you is that correct?"

Sitter: "Oh my god YES! I just talked about it actually on Facebook! He slept with my sisters best friend! She keeps coming on my page to apologize for it but I won't talk to her!"

Psychic: "I'm sorry that happened to you! Now I am also getting that you recently got a new job to! You must feel marvelous with that especially since you just had to stop taking those night courses!"

Sitter: "Yes I am actually! I was shocked that I got it and yes I did have to quit my night courses! I was talking with a friend of mine over on Twitter about it last week in fact!"

▪▪

It is quite simple to see that while the psychic did give some level of validation, they actually cheated with it by researching social media, etc.

This is NOT true validation. This is a highly UNETHICAL PRACTICE, that goes to tarnish true psychics/psychic mediums out there whom are being ethical and honest with their abilities, without feeling the need to cheat in this manner.

A real reading offers true validation in the session between psych and sitter/client. This is where the psychic asks little to no questions, does zero background research on their clients, and is able to provide solid validation by using their own psychic abilities. This is the highest and most purist style of psychic readings. For example:

▪▪

Psychic: "Hi Kenny! I am so glad you are here today!"

Sitter: "Thank you and I am glad to be here as well!"

Psychic: "Now Kenny I'm being told that your aunt recently crossed over recently, like within the last 8 months? Did she go by Kat or Kathy? I keep hearing Kat as a name, but also the name Kathy too."

Sitter: "Yes my aunt Kathleen died almost a year ago. Her friends called her Kathy but I always called her aunt Kit-Kat."

Psychic: "I'm sorry for your loss. Now I am also being shown a modest garden and I hear singing, while I feel like my hands are in moist dirt. I feel like she liked to garden as a hobby and would sing while gardening?"

Sitter: "Yes, she used to sing in her church choir and would also sing while she gardened. She loved planting flowers."

Psychic: "Very good. Thank you. I'm being shown a black knee brace on her left knee? Also being shown here and forgive me for this but, I am being shown her standing in a field of daffodils with her tongue stuck out. She was bit of a wild card wasn't she! She shows me brown hair with a pink strip, on the left side correct?"

Sitter: "Oh wow! Actually yes we all took a family trip out to the country for a reunion and I took a picture of her standing in a field of daffodils! She had a hard time walking because she had twisted her left knee the month earlier and was using a knee brace then too! Also about her hair, I remember my mother being so mad at her for put a hot pink strip on her hair the day before the reunion picture! I laughed so hard then!"

Psychic: (laughs) "OK well please know this is her way of coming through for you today! She sounded like a wonderful woman!"

■■

Now in reading this session, it is easy to see the number of true validations that psychic medium was able to provide to the sitter/client.

This happens when the psychic/psychic medium truly connects with their guides and with those who have crossed over into the afterlife.

This is also known as Evidential Mediumship, where the psychic medium provides solid validation that they have connected to a loved one who has crossed over into the afterlife.

Many reputable psychic/psychic mediums will use Evidential Mediumship during their sessions, this benefits their sitter/clients by means of providing factual, hard core proof (nicknames, personal information, inside jokes, things that only certain people would ever know, etc.) that they have connected with those who have crossed over, thus providing a pleasurable and meaningful session overall.

INTERPRETING SIGNS & MESSAGES

We get signs & messages from our guides and those from the other side around all every minute of the day. The question here is how do we interpret these messages and signs & messages? Do we interpret them literally or symbolically?

Each person, whether it is a psychic medium, or a psychic, or a medium or your average non believing person, has to figure out what works best for them.

When you are a psychic medium, it is important to seek the advice from your guides about messages and signs. Ask them if it is literal or symbolic. This is true for readings, or reading tarot, or dreams, etc.

Personal note here

Myself, when I am reading a photo, I get messages and images. I know those are to be taken literal.

However, the one night I had a dream that my husband and I purchased an old Montessori house and was walking around the yard with someone (there were other people walking around with us). While on our walk…we noticed a huge alligator on the pathway….I mean HUGE. He wasn't friendly. He was chasing several people off the walkway. We just looked and I thought "Wait why is there an alligator in my yard here?!"

Then just last night I was dreaming that my neighbor (here in real life) and I was trying to find out what the heck was making noise in our shared yard. So we turned the flashlights on towards the woods and there was a black bear, quietly eating the leaves from a palm tree. In my dream I even asked "Why is there a black bear here and how did he get on this island?" (I love on an island, in the Florida Keys).

So I knew (after waking up), that I had been given messages symbolically from my guides and that it would be involving both an alligator and a black bear.

While getting ready this morning, I was in the bathroom and BAM! There was a spider near the toilet paper. Ok now I know that whenever I see a spider….that means something drama driven and chaotic hassle like was going to come at me soon.

My guides and I have already figured that out years ago that a spider in a close proximity and personal space (bathroom, etc.) would mean that some sort of drama and chaos would be heading my way.

It wasn't too long after the spider incident that one of my daughters broke up with her boyfriend and begged me to check on him for her. But that I had to be nice. I tried. And I failed. BOOM! Drama and chaos slapped me in the face between him and her. See where I am going with this?

Bottom line it all comes down to communicating with your guides and understanding their messages.

READING NAME/DATE, LOCATIONS & OBJECTS VS. READING FACES

Everything literally has energy in one form or another attached to it. Those who are psychics and psychic mediums, are able to tune in to those energies and read them.

There are four most common areas where energies can be read:
- Faces in a photograph (where the reader is shown an image of a person's face to read)
- Name & Date (where the reader is given a name with a date or just the name to read)
- Locations (where the reader is either present at a specific location, or shown an image of a specific location)
- Objects (where the reader is given an object, that was either held by specific person(s), or has some form of strong history attached to it, etc.)

FACES IN A PHOTOGRAPH:

Many, many psychics and psychic mediums tend to prefer reading an image of a person's face. This is because it tends to visually assist them in the connection overall.

However, as they say looks can be deceiving, especially when it comes to reading people's faces (whether in person or in an image). This is because of three reasons:
- The particular image of a person the reader is viewing is locked in a very specific moment of time. Meaning that they (the subject in the image itself) could have been in a very happy state of mind, or in a very dark place, deep within their soul, or around others whose energies are over-powering their own that time, etc. ESPECIALLY when the subject is part of a crowd, etc.)
- The person has a neutral expression, rendering the reader unable to connect due to lack of facial displays of emotion, body language, etc. (ESPECIALLY those who have careers where facial expressions are not warranted and/or those with detachment issues)
- The "logic noise" part of the readers mind tends to "interpret" the image, thus rendering the reader to make pre-conceived label statements such as: "Appears to be happy", "Seems to love life", "Looks to have had a

hard life", "Looks unhappy or tired", etc.

In order to read the energies connected to a person's face, the reader must push past their logic noise and dig deeper in order to make that strong and clear connection between their energy and that of the person in the photo.

NAME & DATE:

Possessing and strengthening the ability to read energies in a name, either with or without a date is attached, is an ability that is a must for all psychics and psychic mediums.

This is because in many cases (overall), there is no pre-conceived labels of what energy might or might not be present. EXCEPT for those names where logic has already given pre-conceived labels attached to them such as:
• Names that are attached to a specific culture/ethnicity ("Kim Yun Fo"- Asian descent, "Tahar Kamel Amjad" – Arabic Descent, "Eli Virgil Cyrus" – country/hillbilly descent, etc.)
• Names that are pre attached to a specific mental image (such as "Tiffany", "Susie", etc. -a girl who is bubbly, teenager in a mall, pop culture, etc. or "Lucille", "Roberta" - very old names, mostly given to female infants born in the 1930-1960's etc., "Moonbeam Rose", "Gypsy" "Stardust Lavender" – hippy tone names, etc.)

With the exception of some pre-conceived names, reading the energy in names can be more productive overall, simply because the visual side of logic noise does not come into play.

LOCATIONS:

Energies from locations (either in a picture or on site) usually come in two ways:
• Residual Echo's from previous energies that dwelled upon the location (Gettysburg, Trail of Tears, an old house that has had many, many, many occupants over centuries, etc.)
• Present/current energies that have been manifested within a timely manner (a location where a body was discovered or where a crime occurred or any form of strong emotion that recently took place, etc.)

Many (Empathic) psychics and psychic mediums attached to paranormal investigative teams tend to tap into the "residual echo's" of whatever location/residence they are investigating at that time. Location "residual echo's" can reach as far back as centuries and are capable to lasting for many more centuries (depending upon the source of energies, etc.), whereas present day energies can be (usually) connected by all psychics and psychic mediums.

OBJECTS:

All non-living objects are capable of possessing energies from people who have own them for a period of time (case in point haunted and/or cursed dolls, any jewelry, cell phones, clothing, etc.).

A reader can tap into these energies and have the ability to translate information about the person, their personalities, etc. Many psychic detectives also use this ability when assisting law enforcement on criminal cases.

The information received from the object can fluctuate between soft and subtle to extremely profound and direct (depending upon many factors such as what the person was doing while holding the possession, the events surrounding the object, etc.).

REMOVING LOGIC NOISE & LABELS:

Logic noise happens when the logic part of a reader's minds takes over and begins to dictate the defining and labeling of energies. This appears in various forms such as:
- "This person looks happy" (reader looking at a photograph of a person's face)
- "This name sounds ghetto" (reader seeing and/or hearing the name of a person)
- "This place is scary" (reader passing a cemetery)
- "This object is creepy" (reader holding an old ugly doll)

A psychic/psychic mediums job is not to define or label energies with their logic noise. Their job is to connect with energies and relay the messages that they receive as part of that connection.

This is best done by acknowledging two very important factors:
- Everyone has "logic noise" within their minds (same with everyone possessing the same abilities as psychics and psychic mediums. EVERYONE has it, but many do not use it or acknowledge it)
- "Logic noise" is not energy. It labels instead of describes

When a reader first begins to connect with energies in a photograph, or in a name & date, or a location, or with an object, the first few tidbits of information they receive is usually "logic noise".

In order for the reader to effectively receive, they must push through that "logic noise" and establish that true connection from energy to energy, before valid information can come forth.

There is a 4 step process the reader has to take place first and foremost before a true connection can occur:
• Clearing of the mind (means removing all outside disruptions, inner chatter, etc.)
• Asking for true connection and valid information
• Pushing through the "logic noise"
• Focusing the intent & establishing the focus point

The reader must find a focus point first and work outward from there, for instance:
• Photographs of a person's face (focusing on the eyes, instead of the face itself)
• Name & date (focus on the letters in the name itself, instead of images of what the person might look like)
• Location (physically touching the ground (if in person), or focusing on the ground (if in a photograph)
• Object (much like a crystal ball, the reader will want to "stare" into it, going through the many layers, until they come to the center. There is where energies are held the most)

The focus point will always be the primary source of information for all readers.

UNFILTERED PSYCHIC ECHO'S

When you are developing your psychic abilities, it is only natural to have incidents where you experience "unfiltered psychic echo's" whenever you come in contact with various personal items (whether yours, family/friend, old/new, etc.) and/or when you visit different locations (houses, buildings in general, land, etc.)

"Unfiltered psychic echo's" are energies that linger in certain areas. These are (usually) the "first impressions" a psychic experience. The reason they are called "unfiltered psychic echo's" is because they tend to show you (the psychic) all levels of the echo and are often sporadic/chaotic in nature.

CASE EXAMPLE (names changed for privacy):

Kelly is new to his psychic abilities. At the start of a tarot card reading, he requested to use the cards the sitter bought with them. Instead of reading for the sitter in front of him, he began to relay the "unfiltered echo's" attached to the cards.

He relayed about how the sitter was an avid drug user and how there have been previous law enforcement encounters, issues with bad lovers, etc. All in which were 100% wrong. This created frustration on both sides.

The sitter elected to take back her cards and offer Kelly her ring instead to read. The reading from the ring was not only 100% different, but was overall approximately 60% correct. Still much of his reading was based on the "unfiltered echo's".

Afterwards, it occurred to the sitter, that the tarot card deck she bought to the session had actually been given to her by an acquaintance. While she knew this person, she did not know them well. This prompted her to learn more about that person. The result was that Kelly had tapped into that person's unfiltered psychic echo's.

After learning this, the sitter decided to re-program the tarot deck, so that only their energies were attached.

While most of these can be best described as "fleeting glimpses of energies", there are some that are so intense to where all of the senses are included, to where it can lasts for several minutes and can be quite vivid.

It is important to mention here that many psychic empaths, who are newly joined to a paranormal team and are on their first investigation, can actually disrupt the investigation to a great extent by experiencing these "unfiltered echo's".

To those who are considering joining a paranormal team (or if your team is considering accepting a psychic/psychic medium/empath), it is strongly urged that care is taken.

Experiencing "unfiltered echo's" is quite similar to having psychic ADHD…because the energies are unfiltered and chaotic, this results in the reading being chaotic and unorganized overall.

It is strongly urged that the psychic/psychic medium/empath be bought in separately and with one (perhaps two at most) members to record their reading. This is because the electrical energies from the equipment can also enhance the strength of the "unfiltered echo's".

CASE EXAMPLE (names changed for privacy):

Lisa is a psychic medium/empath. She joins a local paranormal team and attends her first investigation. They are investigating a reported residential haunting.

Lisa is bought in at the start of the investigation. As she walks from room to room, she becomes distracted with vast levels of "unfiltered echo's", combined with the electrical energies stemming from the numerous investigative equipment (video recorders, t.v.'s, laptops, EVP readers, etc.), she feels as if she is on a sugar/caffeine rush and begins to derail the investigation overall as she is consumed by the "unfiltered echo's soon.

Her chaos with the "unfiltered echo's" spilled over to the rest of the team…making everyone feel like they were also on a sugar rush, as well as being all over the board per say.

The investigation was shut down after an hour. Through careful examination of everything, it was deemed that Lisa's abilities needed to be re-evaluated to see where they can be best used by the team effectively, if at all.

So the question here is how can a psychic/psychic medium/empath effectively work through the "unfiltered echo's"?

These steps are recommended:
• Regulate your "internal circuit board system": Keep your pulse, heartbeat, breathing calm and even
  • Clear your mind: Focus only on what is vital
  • Learn the difference between "unfiltered echo's" and the actual energies you need to tap into: (This is hard for many who are new to their abilities) EVERYONE will experience this, but the key is to acknowledge and work past them, so that you can then tap into the true source (meaning you have to dig deeper several layers, psychically speaking)
  • Refrain from sugar/caffeine prior to the session: This will assist in keeping you calmer and more able to focus on the task at hand
  • Limit the amount of electronic devices interference: Turn cell phones

off, if you are performing a paranormal investigation, request that all electronic devices not only be turned off, but unplugged during the investigation (if you are located outside, steer clear from electric and/or phone lines etc.)

• Remove your shoes: This might sound weird, but if you can manage to keep your bare feet connected to the ground, it aides in grounding the chaotic energies, thus shielding you somewhat better as well

Remember…as a psychic/psychic medium/empath…you are actually a conduit for energies.

MAINTIANING YOUR EMOTIONAL DISTANCE AS AN EMPATH (DURING READING SESSIONS)

When you are an Empath, the world can (sometimes) become an over-stimulated plane of existence.

If you are a psychic medium Empath, both worlds (the living and the afterlife) can become quite overly stimulated, thus throwing you into a wild tail-spin (at times). It's hard to figure out where their emotions end and yours begin.

Some emotions that are most difficult to maintain (as an Empath) are as follows:
• Sadness
• Anger
• Sexual feelings

The last thing a psychic medium ever wants is for the client has to console them instead of the psychic medium consoling the client:

▪▪▪

Psychic medium: I'm getting a little boy who crossed over by way of a fire. He looks to be about 7 years old perhaps. He says his name is Bobby.

Client: Yes, that is my son. His name was Robert, but we called him Bobby. He died around 10 years ago in a fire.

Psychic medium: He shows me those small white flowers you see all over…those small white flowers with the yellow center. He says you used to call them vanilla cups?

Client: (gets teary) Yes. Those would be similar to the buttercups. They are weeds but I used to call them vanilla cups….similar to the buttercups. We used to pick them and throw them up in the air and let them fall around us…

Psychic medium: (starts to feel tears and gets choked up): He talks about his last birthday and how you picked a handful of those flowers, sorry weeds (chokes back more tears) and how you threw them up in the air then twirled around as they fell around you. He said that he liked it a lot and that he loves you and misses you- (tears start flowing freely)

Client: (Reaches over) It's ok! I'm ok with this reading! You can continue!

Psychic medium: (shakes her head as she sobs): No! He was such a sweet little boy! The flowers meant so much to him! Oh he loved you so much! I just feel so bad that he died in that fire! Oh this is so painful!

∎∎

The session has now stopped. What once was a mediumship session, it has actually now turned into where the client has to console the psychic medium.

Connecting and displaying some level of emotional connection is vital for a productive session, however allowing yourself to become overly emotional, to where the client needs to stop their session and console you is not only unprofessional, but unfair to the client, because it takes away from their connection, their healing and their validation overall.

(At times) It can be difficult to maintain your emotional distance during sessions (especially if you are an Empath).

When you are in a sensitive session and you feel yourself becoming overly sensitive to the messages you are receiving (whether verbally or seeing images, etc.), you need to pause and ask yourself (and your guides!) these two questions:
• How can I push through this moment without losing my composure?
• Am I able to push through this moment without losing my composure?

If you find that you are unable to complete the session without losing your composure, then politely and gently explain to the client that you must take a break for a few moments, then politely stand up and go get some air.

While you are getting fresh air, try these steps:
• Close your eyes and try inhaling deeply (and slowly) a few times through your nose, and exhaling slowly through your mouth
• Visualize yourself in a safe, peaceful and soothing place (create it in your mind). Stay there quietly for a few moments
• Open your eyes, keep your mind there. Have your guides transport the spirits to you, where you can maintain your control
• Upon returning to the session, take a deep breath and resume the

connection

If, for some reason, the visualization fails to deter you from becoming overly emotional, then you are faced with the possibility of rescheduling the session entirely until you are able to move forth.

The biggest key to all sessions is to remember that the sessions are not about you and your emotions. They are about:
- The client and their emotions/messages
- The person, who has crossed over and their emotions/messages

It is always good to be compassionate, but it is never good to become so overly emotionally distraught to where the client has to stop their session and take care of you.

WHEN TO SHARE SENSITIVE INFORMATION AND HOW TO HANDLE THE SELF BLAME GAME

One of the main questions I get from students is "When do I know it is ok to share sensitive information with a person?"

My standard advice is for them to gauge whether or not the person in question would be open to receive this form of sensitive information, in addition to, if they aren't, then 3 questions need to be answered:
- Is this person important enough in my life to share this information regardless of their views and opinions of psychic mediums?
- How important is this information exactly? Is it life changing?
- Are you prepared for whatever is given to you as a response from this person?

PERSONAL STORY

A few years ago, my guides gave me a "Practice what you preach" lesson one day. My husband was away on a deployment (Afghanistan) and I was helping our yard guy, Stan, put in a new door on our back porch.

Within a few moments, a vision hit me. I saw Stan falling out of a huge tree, with a running chainsaw.

Needless to say it unnerved me. Stan had been working for us for almost a year and I dearly loved this man. He was quirky, outspoken to a fault, very "Northerner" as opposed to my southern style and while at times we clashed somewhat on opinions, we definitely had formed a strong bond of friendship.

Anyhow, I felt a sense of panic as a wave of vision flowed over me again, to where I had to lean against the wall and close my eyes for a moment. Stan, being Stan, thought I needed to get something to drink (it was rather hot outside).

I went and got a glass of water then returned to watch him for a second. Then took a deep breath and decided to share with him what I saw and hoped that he listened to me.

What transpired was me getting chewed out up and down by this 64 year old man. Scolding me for believing in "That poppycock nonsense that only a child would believe in."

To say that I felt as if I was a child at that moment was a great understatement. For a few awkward moments, there was an uncomfortable silence that hung in the air.

I quickly made an excuse of having to go do laundry, in order to get away. Just before leaving, I gave last plea of "Stan regardless of your views please do not climb any trees today with a chainsaw!" then asked him if he wanted me to get him anything while I was out.

He half barked at me that he was too busy with my porch stairs that he built himself and my plants to be messing around with any chainsaws that day.
As I started to leave he half waved at me and asked that I get him a pop (soda).
I lingered at some stores after my laundry, dreading going home and facing Stan, fearing he would still chastise me on some level. Basically I was feeling as if I was a child.

I got home right around dusk, I didn't see Stan. I marveled at the door and my new steps, while talking with my dog groomer (who also was a good friend of mine and who also thought psychic stuff was a waste of time and only meant for idiots) on my cell, when this elderly woman came up to my fence and asked if my name was Sue and if I knew Stan.

I nodded and asked why then dropped my phone as I heard "There has been an accident. Stan was trimming my tree on top of my roof and he slipped and fell with the chainsaw."

I felt as if I had been punched in the stomach, as I asked if he fell on the chainsaw. He had not, but wasn't responsive. He had been flown to Miami trauma and that nobody knew anything else at that time.

I went back and grabbed my phone. I called my friend back and told her what happened. Her response was "Ok that is terrible but it isn't like you shoved him off the roof right?"

I won't lie, that question shot through me like a bullet. I made an excuse to get off the phone and quickly went inside to sit down. The only thing that went through my mind over and over was the question "It isn't like you shoved him of the roof right?"

Stan stayed in ICU for three months. His heart has stopped twice during the flight. He had broken his neck and would forever be paralyzed and relying on a respirator.

My husband soon came home and after I broke down and cried about what happened, he said we needed to go visit Stan. I refused. I panicked.

What if he remembered that day and blamed me? What if he gets so angry at me that he strokes out and dies in front of me? And the biggest question that refused to leave my mind "Was this really my fault? Did I unwittingly suggest to him that he would fall?"

My husband, being of logic, but understanding my world now (after 20+ years), forced me to go. He said we owed it to Stan and that it would be beneficial for all of us.

The drive to the hospital is four hours each direction (we live in the islands), on the way there, I begged my guides for strength and guidance. All I got back was "Breathe"

We arrived at the hospital and made our way to his room. There was a sign in sheet there, gloves, cape, etc. His family was there as well (his daughters and his mother, who was in a wheelchair). And there was Stan, hooked up to machines and I.V.'s.

His family greeted us and we chatted for a few moments outside in the hallways, each taking a few moments to go see him.

When it was my time, I grabbed my husband hand and asked him to go with me. I was literally shaking and I couldn't decide if I was going to burst into tears, throw up, or faint (knowing my luck, it probably would have been all three if I had to go in alone).

We went in and Stan saw me. He gave me a soft smile and motioned with his eyes for me to come closer. Gently I did and leaned in to say hi to him and ask how he was. He said he was fine, just being lazy. He made a joke! I felt my spirits go up somewhat hearing his response and giggled.

I then asked him if he remembered anything about that day. He closed his eyes and mouthed "No." A deep sense of relief covered me like a warm blanket as I fought to keep the tears from flowing.

We stayed for a few more minutes, then said our goodbyes and left. In the safety of our car, I broke down and sobbed like a child. I felt a buffet table of emotions, ranging from remorse, guilt, anger, confusion to exhaustion and relief.

I decided not to do any readings, or teach anyone until I could effectively process the accident, my role and my responses from everything.

We made it to see Stan twice more, then one night, as I was coming home from a late night photo shoot, I saw and heard Stan in my backyard, cutting some wood, telling me that he was going to fix my front steps rail then work on my grass.

I knew that was a visit from him. I smiled and nodded as I went inside my home.

Later that next morning I received a call from a friend telling me that Stan has passed away the night before.

I saw that elderly woman once more after learning of Stan's death and asked her if she was ok and how did she know Stan.

She explained that she was a widow and Stan would often pop over to help her out. On that particular day, she noticed him working on my back porch and asked if he could come over to trim a few trees for her. He said yes after he finished up with my new stairs he built.

I viewed this as a learning experience from my guides. Although in all honestly, I wished they had chosen a different path to enlighten me.

If you were to ask me if I would change anything in my telling Stan about my vision, I would say no. I felt then as I do now, that it was important enough and he was important enough for me to risk everything and warn him.

8 SETTING BOUNDARIES

SETTING YOUR BOUNDARIES AS A MEDIUM

There comes a time in your experiences as a medium where you encounter three types of profound experiences:
• You are unable to go to a certain place, because you feel as if you are being over-crowded and/or pulled in a hundred different directions (tons of chatter, chaos, etc.)
• You become the token "doctor at the cocktail party" with someone/group of people (they call/text/etc. you constantly with every little bump that happens in the night, they think they are haunted (or possessed) and only you can help soothe their nerves, they ask you endless questions about their future/their family members (dead and alive)/their health/etc.).
• Spirits from the other-side seem to invade your space 24/7 (trust me it can happen).

When any of the above three incidents occur (or all three of them), Your body and psyche start giving you signals:
• Headaches (anywhere from dull/mild ache to a full blown migraine throb)
• Losing patience quickly (your tolerance level greatly decreases)
• Feeling over-whelmed
• Physical pain (eyes hurt, muscle ache, etc.
• Sleepy/exhausted (feeling as if you can just crawl into bed and sleep the rest of the day away, etc.)
• Wanting to be "left alone to sit quietly for a while"

The solution is to establish boundaries and stick to them.

The first experience (entering a certain place and feeling over-crowded, being pulled into a hundred different directions, etc.) can and does occur (even to the most experienced, the most shielded, the most grounded, etc.). The best way to resolve that is:
• To acknowledge that a certain place or places will have a certain effect on you
• Limit your time in that certain place
• Have a distraction for you (a book, music, a game, etc.)
• After being at that certain place, go for a soothing/peaceful walk outside in nature (if you can tolerate it and if weather permits, go barefoot, it helps you ground back to the earth and the sensation of the grass not only stimulates your feet, but feels soothing overall)
• Upon returning home, grab a hot shower and change your clothing (the energy from that area can attach to you, so make sure you wash them before wearing them again)

The second experience (becoming the token "doctor at a cocktail party" occurs when your well-meaning friends/family members get excited to learn that you are a medium and they come to you with every little incident, every question, at all hours of the day & night.

They also invite you over all the time or to lunch with their other friends and introduce you as "This is my friend, she/he can talk to the dead! Go on! Ask them about someone who died!"

As well-meaning as they are and as close as the two of you may be, if this is allowed to continue, you will feel as if you are only wanted because of you being a medium (and thus, places the relationship in danger).

The best and only way to resolve this is to sit them down and discuss this with love and honestly (but most of all be clear).

Establish basic rules/guidelines (for the sake of the relationship) that works for the both of you and doesn't impede the relationship or your being a medium.

The third and final experience deals directly with spirits who bombard you 24/7. They are in your dreams, they are in the front part of your mind, you can hear them, you can see them, you can feel them.

The reason this happens is because when you first become open to the other side, it is as if the flood gates open up and your mind is open, constantly processing information. This is actually pretty normal (again everyone goes through this at one time or another).

The best way to deal with this situation is by two ways:
• Incorporate your guides and tell them to assist in blocking them during certain times (sleeping, personal time, etc.)
• Telling those from the other-side to "Stop", "Go Away", "Not Right Now!" (visualize you hanging a "Closed" sign during certain times and leave it until you are ready to "open" for business again)

Establishing healthy boundaries is vital for a healthy, fulfilling life overall (whether it is spiritual, non-spiritual, etc.)

By establishing healthy boundaries (and sticking to them), you will soon discover that chaotic situations/people/etc. will fall away.

This is a win-win situation for yourself and the world around you.

HANDLING THE "BUT WE'RE FRIENDS/FAMILY SYNDROME"

When you decide to step away from behind the curtain and let others know that you are a psychic medium, you will begin to get bombarded by well meaning (and eager) friends and/or family members who will no doubt come to you with ALL of their drama, ALL of their relationship questions, ALL of their employment questions, etc.

No matter how many times you have given them advice, they always seem to go in the OPPOSITE direction (free will gets them every time it seems like). But after a while this starts to get old and the following side effects appear in you:
• You start feeling drained around them/tired/lack of energy/sense of dread, etc.
• You feel yourself becoming snappish and short around them (irritable)
And in extreme cases:
• You start to avoid them/their calls/etc.

■■■

Case example between two friends:
Medium picks up her phone: Hello?
Friend: Kathy I need to come over right now and ask you some questions girl!
Medium (rolls her eyes and sighs): I'm about to go out to the store-
Friend: It will ONLY take a few moments! Can I stop over when you

get back? How long will you be?!

Medium (shakes her head and sighs): Ok come over right now. BUT! I have to go somewhere soon and don't have a lot of patience for whatever guy issue you seem to have this time!

(within a few moments her friend comes over and quickly barges in holding something)

Friend: Ok so I have been dating this guy I met a few weeks ago kinda on the side-

Medium: On the side of what?????

Friend (giggles): Geesh aren't you a psychic? Doesn't this stuff just come to you?

Medium (sighs and shakes her head then sits down): What did you need?

Friend (reaches in a bag and pulls out an article of clothing and tries to hand it to the Medium): Here. Hold these and tell me what you get!

Medium (eyes bulge out as she wrinkles her face): What the hell is that? UNDERWEAR?! Did you take his UNDERWEAR and EXPECT ME TO READ THEM FOR YOU?!

Friend (confused): Well he left them over at my place last night! They are clean! I checked! I wouldn't hand you nasty underwear! I just need you-

Medium (snaps as she gets up and walks to her kitchen): No what you need to do is get that away from me BEFORE you have to explain to a E.R. Doctor WHY you have a black eye crazy woman!

(And argument breaks out for a few moments, then the medium gives in against her wishes)

Medium: I can't believe I am DOING this! Fine! Give me his nasty drawers, sit down and shut up!

The friend sits down eagerly as the medium holds the underwear and focuses.

Medium: Ok what did you want to know?

Friend (babbles all at once): Is he married? Is he a baby daddy? Does he have a good job? Can he help pay my bills?

(Medium stands up, throws the underwear down, then marches over to her front door and opens it angrily)

Medium (in a stern voice): GET OUT!!!!! I'm done! Seriously! I am no longer your low jack on every loser you hook up with down the line!

Friend (stands up, feeling upset an angry): But-but-but Kathy we're friends! Why are you so angry at me now? What did I do?! I support your powers! I look at you for advice-

Medium (shakes her head gently shoves her friend out of the door): Not anymore! I'm done! Don't call me don't come by, you know just FORGET me 100%!!!!!

This is a true story that actually happened between a previous friend of mine and myself.

She was forever coming to me for advice. She was forever getting herself into ridiculous situations and in spite of every advice I gave her (I know, I know, free will...but come on...use some level of common sense right?), she still chose to run head first into drama and chaos.

Because we were such very close friends, I allowed her to use me in this fashion. BUT after a while of her constant using me as her personal low jack to hidden information, etc. I found myself losing my temper with her more and more frequently.

Finally the day came (the same incident with the BVD's) to where I simply lost it on her.

In this case example, I toned down a LOT of my language with her that day and yes, I ended up really hurting her feelings, and yes our friendship was severed that day.

A few weeks later we actually crossed paths at an event. It was surface friendly at best, but the true bond between us was forever gone.

The lesson I learned from this was that I had to establish boundaries and stick to them.

When it comes to friends (especially close friends) and/or families, we tend to give them extra lead way to get away with a lot more than the average stranger on the street. While this is understandable, it can (and often does) cause issues, if this behavior is allowed to continue.

So what can you do?

Sometimes the best advice is to let them walk their path on their own and if (or when) they fall, be there to support them, (in a hands off style).

Doing it this way isn't easy nor is it fun to watch someone you love and care about go down a path you already know is a disaster, but it will save you from pulling out your own hair and possibly severing a relationship.

We each have a path to walk on and lessons to learn. Some lessons will need to be learned the hard way before the person actually learns the lesson.

WHEN THE SPIRITS STILL LINGERS AFTER A SESSION

There comes a time in every psychic medium career when a spirit lingers after a session. When this happens, it is (usually) because of one of two reasons:
1. They still have messages for their loved ones (or to another specific person)
2. They have established a connection with you as the medium and enjoy sharing their favorite memories with you

When a spirit has more messages for their loved ones (or for a specific person, i.e.: Law Enforcement, etc.), they will (usually) provide you with messages specifically geared for that person, for example:
• Private joke that only the spirit and that person would understand
• Movies, extra special celebrations that (again) only the spirit and that person would remember
• Personal and specific details surrounding a situation that only they (the spirit) would know (this happens most often in criminal acts)

These messages, etc. can go on for days after the initial session. The question is what do you do with these messages? You have two choices:
• Journal them, then relay them to the specific person
• Ignore them (but understand that if you do ignore it, it won't make them move on anytime soon)

The other reason why a spirit would linger after a session is because they have established a connection with you and therefore want to share more of themselves with you (think of it as having a new bestie for a few days).

When this happens, they tend to share literally everything about themselves to you, such as:
• What their favorite foods/color/t.v. show/season/holiday/hobbies, etc. were during their lifetime
• Their personal favorite memories

Notice the difference between the two styles…the first one was geared more towards a specific person, whereas the second is geared more towards themselves on a very intimate level.

Often this happens for no other reason than they (the spirit) enjoy sharing their special memories with you.

Sprits like it when we (the living) are open to receive, because it gives them the opportunity to share what means a lot to them with someone from the living.

So what should you do when you have these types of encounters? Nothing except smile and enjoy the fact that you have been chosen to receive a very special gift of friendship from the other side.

The main question many new psychics asks is should they help them (the spirit) cross over after a session?

The answer isn't always black and white.

In many instances spirits will move on when they are ready to move on. If they have messages to pass on, and they are passed on, then a lot of time, they will move on.

If they linger and share personal memories and such with the medium for several days, then it is up to the medium to decide how long this can continue.

Ordinarily, these situations only lasts for a few days, then the spirit moves on (or sometimes they may come and go but won't really be a bothersome).

If the medium wishes, they can simply advise the spirit that it is time to go.

The main thing in any situation is for the psychic medium to establish healthy boundaries ahead of time and make sure they are adhered to from both side (the living and the dead).

9 SKEPTICS AND DEBRIEFING AFTER A READING

DEALING WITH SKEPTICS

We've all had them in one form or another, concerning any number of conversations ranging from whether or not we actually walked on the moon, validity of evolution, even to the existence of the paranormal (throw in various variations as to whether or not Elvis is still alive somewhere).

A skeptic is defined as a person who questions the validity or authenticity of something purporting to be factual. Quite simply, they chose not to believe in something for whatever reason, even when the proof is over whelming factual.

As a psychic medium, you will no doubt encounter one or two or a herd of them. So what do you do when you encounter a skeptic? Do you argue your side till blue in the face? No that would only fan the flames and end the end would give you (and others around you) a headache. Do you present "factual evidence" to prove those from the other side can and often do communicate with us in the living?

No. Why? Simple, they would simply elect not to believe it from you. So then how do you get around a skeptic?

First, respect their point of views. Nobody said you have to agree (or even like them) with them. But you do have to respect them.

Second, you embrace their skepticism. You also take the time right then and there to accept the reality that until they choose that they are ready and open to accept the fact that those from the other side can and often do communicate with the living, there is very little to nothing at all that can be done to flip that switch. No "magic reading" from Uncle Henry will change that either until the person themselves make that decision.

Now, there are two basically types of skeptics that you, as a psychic medium will encounter:
• Those who live strictly in the scientific world (basically all these guys want is 100% scientific proof, that was scientifically conducted in a scientifically controlled environment, over a course of years and factual scientific case studies are not only proven, but well documented in books and Universities)
And/or…
• Those who want a reading, get a reading, get solid proof during the reading and will still say "Nope. Nope. Nope.", only then to go outside to their cars, to call their best friend and, not only talk about how awesome the reading was, but how factual it was.

Having a skeptic around you is actually healthy. They assist in keeping you grounded and more aware of your gifts, as a psychic medium. They will force you to evaluate yourself and the messages which you receive and pass on to others. They will force you to step back sometimes and become a skeptic on yourself and others, who also share your gifts.

Our job is not to change them or their thought patterns/beliefs, or even to attempt to "WOW" them with a profound reading, etc. But to understand that they are simply not ready to accept your version of reality and the color of your sky.

Now if, by chance, they do come around to your line of thinking and are receptive to believing in your gifts or others like you, then that is pure gravy. But if not, don't get upset, don't engage in debate, don't try to sway them over to your side.

But embrace them. Acknowledge their right to have their opinions and respect their right to have their opinions and keep being true to yourself and your guides.

For example, I had a client bring his friend along once for a reading (at that time I was doing readings at a little health food store). As soon as the two came towards me, I instantly felt this strong resistance and resentment literally oozing from this guy.

I asked for the mans watch to hold (by which he retorted "Why so you can hock it later, won't get you much, just a cheap piece of shit"). I chuckled briefly, and began to read him.

Every statement I made was met with variations of "No", "Nope wrong again.", "Naw huh", "Sorry but no.", "I don't know."

I could tell that my client (his friend) was getting anxious, biting his tongue to keep from saying something. But he remained silent.

After the reading, the friend stood up and said to his friend "You just blew your money on nothing bro." and walked away.

I began to gather my things, when my client leaned over and said "I'm real sorry about him. He just isn't open and I shouldn't have brought him here. By the way, you were right about many points. Why he didn't said that is beyond me."

I smiled and patted my clients hand as I reassured him that his friend was OK and that when he is ready to accept a different form of reality then he will at that time and that I was not offended nor upset.

So the next time you encounter a skeptic, acknowledge it, respect it and move on.

DEBRIEFING AFTER A SESSION (ESPECIALLY AN INTENSE SESSION)

Giving a psychic medium reading session is (usually) always productive and energetic. Both sides (the sitter and the reader) are filled with energy. This is a good thing. This aides in the transference of messages from those who have crossed over.

But what does the psychic medium do with this energy after a session? What about if the session is an intense session and the energy is so intense, to where the psychic medium can feel as if they are on an overload of caffeine? What happens of the energy is not released? What are some of the drawbacks?

A strong connection to those who have crossed over can often be felt in a psychical sense such as:
- A buzzing in your ears
- That "rush" feeling as if you are on a roaring roller coaster

- "Bouncy" feeling (sometimes swinging your legs/feet under the table, etc.)
- Tingling/tickling/fluttering in and around your chakras (especially your third eye & your solar plexus)
- Some psychic mediums experience extreme thirst (or a drying of throat as well in some cases)

During the session, the psychic medium can also feel whatever emotions, etc. they receive from those who have crossed over too (whether the messages come from pleasant and/or unpleasant emotions, etc.).

Once the session has ended some may experience:
- Hunger
- Thirsty
- Headache
- Sleepy/drained
- A "coating" on their skin and clothes

A recommendation to assist in resolving these feelings are as follows:
- Break the spiritual connection who those who have crossed over (this is extremely important)
- Get a shower (first as hot as you can handle, suds up really good, then rinse off with warm, then give a blast of semi cold water and let it flow over your body)
- Lean against the shower wall, close your eyes and simply exhale a few times as you imagine the emotions, spiritual connections, etc. flowing off of you and down into the drain
- Wear fresh clothing (do not wear the same clothing if possible & nothing tight/confining, etc.)
- Smudge (sage) your area
- Light fresh incense (not the same fragrance as you had during the session if you had any)
- Eat a light meal (take your time eating, enjoy each taste and flavor)
- Listen to music (can be any type of music that appeals to you)
- Do something fun (go for a brief walk, play a game, dance, etc.)
- Go to bed early (some say that this is the most helpful)

An additional note to the who utilize crystals & other props during the session, they also need to be "cleansed" and "rejuvenated". This can be done by the following process:
- Gently wipe each tool/prop with a warm cloth
- Smudge/sage
- Stick in a freezer overnight (if possible)

- Sit out in direct moonlight or sunlight for a few hours

The key here is to completely separate yourself from the session and give some much needed nourishment back to yourself (in every sense possible).

SIGNS OF DEPLEATING YOUR WELL & HOW TO REPLENISH YOUR SOUL

More often than not, when we find something that gives us warm fuzzies (passionate, vibrant, a zest and/or gusto for life, etc.), a physical and psychological transformation starts to take place.

We begin to feel euphoric in nature, little "ah-ha" moments happen and we feel as if we were meant to experience this at that time and much like a child eating Christmas cookies, we do not want to stop anytime soon LOL!

It isn't long before we start seeing/feeling that we have perhaps crossed that invisible line of "passion overload". When that starts to happen, our bodies and mind start sending us signals for us to slow down and re balance ourselves once more.
- Mild headache
- Feeling sluggish
- Not feeling as if you get enough sleep
- Minor digestive issues

Now if we fail to acknowledge those signals, then things kick into overdrive and our lives become more stressful and we are left with questions, confusion and (perhaps) discomfort/anger.
- Nagging headache (migraine level at times)
- Lack of appetite/unhealthy eating habits (binge junk food eater)
- Moderate to severe sleep related issues, not sleeping well, restless sleep
- Easily irritable and shows signs of impatience/frustration/feelings of being "over whelmed"
- Unable to process conversations in general/forgets things easily/distracted
- (Sometimes) Flu like symptoms, achy, feeling "off balance", lethargic, etc.

Our bodies and spirit is much like a well. If we continue to take from the well, without refilling that well, then we deplete ourselves.

No matter what our passion is (especially if you are opening yourself up as a psychic medium, etc.), it is vital that you understand what your body and spirit (not the outside spirits but rather the one inside of you LOL!) is trying to relay to you. It is important to always important to give back to yourself and replenish yourself on a daily basis. This is a must (especially if you are just opening yourself up to working with energies).

Some of the best ways to do this is:
• Taking a brief ten minute walk (not a speed walk, but more of a relaxing walk around your block, look at things outside, clear your mind, leave that list of things back at the house and don't think about it while you are on your walk).
• Cut off everything electronic in your home about fifteen15 minutes prior to going to bed and listen to the silence. Enjoy the silence. Take it in. It (the silence) has a way of assisting in healing your soul after a long day (believe it or not).
• Take at least one meal a day, and enjoy it. Enjoy the textures, the taste, if you cook, enjoy that process of making it by hand. Take your time with it (don't rush, this is your time to enjoy this meal).
• Exhale as you get settled in bed at night and close your eyes (exhaling is a way of telling your mind and body "Ok this is enough for right now"
• Find something "fun" to do everyday for ten minutes (great way to find your inner child)
• Sprinkle lavender scented baby powder on your mattress just prior to placing fresh sheets on your bed, also place your clean sheet set in your freezer for a few moments before placing them on the bed, then make the bed tight. Later, when you get into your bed, you smell the lavender, feels the softness from the baby powder, mixed with the slight coolness of the sheets (this is an excellent way to ease yourself back into a peaceful sleep).

Xoxox Always remember to replenish your well xoxox

10 FINAL THOUGHTS

Being a psychic medium has always been a treasure in my eyes. I do feel like I have blessed by a high power to do what I do and see what I see.

I've met some truly magical and impressive souls (both living and those who have crossed over) along the way, while also created beautiful memories that will stay with me throughout my existence.

I know my journey isn't done yet…

Not by far.

It is my most sincere hope that you as well shall carry on your spiritual path and that you may also encounter beautiful souls and create some truly magnificent memories along the way.

Always remember that all of us are on a journey and that our paths cross for a reason…that is reason in to love and help each other learn about whom we are and what makes us special.

Be real…

Be blessed…

Be…

You.

~ Sue M. Swank ~

ABOUT THE AUTHOR

Sue M. Swank is a wife, mother, grandmother, author, photographer and a psychic medium.

She came into her abilities as a young child and while on her spiritual path, she has not only managed to learned how to work with her own abilities, but has also helped others, who were struggling or curious on their own individual paths as well.

In her spare time. Sue enjoys a variety of activities such as being outdoors and relaxing with her family.

Currently, Sue is enjoying the laid back tropical life in the Florida Keys, with her husband and her dog, Chance.

Sue encourages communication with her fans and is always eager to make new friends…connect with her up today on the internet!

EMAIL: keywestswank@aol.com
Facebook Page: https://www.facebook.com/psychicmediumsuesank
Twitter: https://twitter.com/sueswank
Website: http://www.psychicmediumsueswank.com
Blog: https://psychicmediumsueswank.wordpress.com

Printed in Great Britain
by Amazon